MONOLOGUES FROM CLASSIC PLAYS
468 B.C. – 1960 A.D.

Jocelyn A. Beard has edited:

The Best Men's Stage Monologues of 1991
The Best Women's Stage Monologues of 1991
The Best Men's Stage Monologues of 1990
The Best Women's Stage Monologues of 1990
One Hundred Men's Stage Monologues from the 1980's
One Hundred Women's Stage Monologues from the 1980's

and has co-edited:

The Best Stage Scenes for Men from the 1980's
The Best Stage Scenes for Women from the 1980's

David Esbjornson is the Artistic Director of the Classic Stage
Company.

Other Books for Actors from Smith and Kraus

If you require pre-publication information about upcoming Smith and Kraus monologue collections, scene collections, play anthologies, advanced acting books, and books for young actors, you may receive our semi-annual catalogue, free of charge, by sending your name and address to Smith and Kraus Catalogue, P.O. Box 10, Newbury, VT 05051.

MONOLOGUES FROM CLASSIC PLAYS
468 B.C. TO 1960 A.D.

Edited by
Jocelyn A. Beard

SK
A Smith and Kraus Book

A Smith and Kraus Book
Published by Smith and Kraus, Inc.

Manufactured in the United States of America

First Edition: December, 1992
10 9 8 7 6 5 4 3 2 1

Library of Congress Cataloging-in-Publication Data

Monologues From classic plays, 486 B.C. - 1960 A.D. / edited by Joeclyn A.
Beard ; introduction by David Esbjornson.
    p. cm. -- (The Monologue audition series)
  ISBN 1-880399-09-1 : $11.95
  1. Acting. 2. Monologues. 3. Drama--Translations into English.
4. English drama. 5. American drama. I. Beard, Jocelyn.
II. Series.
PN2080.M542 1993
808.82'45--dc20   92-36194
                                            CIP

Smith and Kraus, Inc.
Main Street, P.O. Box 10, Newbury, Vermont 05051
(802) 866 5423

iv

ACKNOWLEDGMENTS

I would like to thank my wonderful husband Kevin Kitowski.

MONOLOGUES FROM CLASSIC PLAYS
468 B.C. - 1960 A.D.

Table of Contents

Men's Monologues:

Women's Monologues

FOREWORD

When contemplating the compilation of a collection of classic monologues, I kept the following definition in mind:

> *"classics: any body of work of the first or highest order. The term comes from the Roman division of society into five classes. Any citizen who belonged to the highest class was called classicus; the rest were said to be infra classem, that is, beneath the class."*
>
> **Benet's Reader's Encyclopedia**
> **Third Edition**

Rest assured that there are no infra classem selections to be found within the pages of this book, for every effort has been made to include works of a truly classic nature. The ages of world theatre are all well represented, including pieces from classical Greece and Rome, Medieval European morality plays, the Restoration period, the Romantic period, 20th Century Theatre of the Absurd and works from the post-war era.

This book has been assembled to give you - the actor - a unique understanding of the development of men's and women's roles over the past 2300 years of theatre history. In your career you will undoubtedly be required to portray countless types of people, from ancient to modern. This book will give you a jump on things by presenting you with the very best of every conceivable type.

Beginner and veteran alike will here discover a treasure trove of useful material that will help to enrich your insight into the complex nature of role portrayal as well as your interest in classical theatre. At the very least, it is my hope that meeting some of the colorful and dynamic characters represented in this book may finally persuade you to read a play that you've always been meaning to, but haven't had the time. Researching this book was a humbling experience that rekindled my respect for the world's great playwrights. Hopefully, reading this book will do the same for you.

Break a leg!

Jocelyn A. Beard
Patterson, NY
Autumn 1992

INTRODUCTION

Congratulations on your choice of audition text. I think you will find that you have chosen an excellent collection of material for your classical monologues needs. What makes introducing these pieces so pleasurable, is that I know what kind of challenge they provide. These pages are rich with information and there is so much to be gained by a personal investigation of their secrets.

As always the audition process seems to be a contradiction in terms. Where is the process in a system that seems to be less about one's ability to develop a character and more about some immediate and often superficial impression? And yet the classical text provides the clearest indication of an actors' ability and their personal connection to the work. The rigorous demands of language style and historical knowledge can be absolutely revealing, making it one of the most difficult challenges for a theatre artist. With out a clear and comprehensive approach even the most gifted actor is in danger of missing an important discovery that can give that necessary advantage.

We have all heard the expression "the play is the thing" and there is no question that the text is the tangible road map for all the work we do. Read the entire play -- not just the monologue. Try to discover the voice at the center of the play. What is the playwright's connection to the world at that precise moment in time? What is his/her social position and what are the political circumstances that have formed their impressions? You will need to note the appropriate code of behavior of that time, realizing of course that strong dramatic literature often shows people in the midst of breaking social mores. This conflict is critical because it is often the basis of the character's dramatic truth and your emotional access to it. Discovering parallels between yourself and the past are often surprising and can help you access specific character choices. It is seldom necessary to look for added emotion or theatricality. The clues in the text will give you strong clear signals about breathing, rhythm, intonation and intention. Think of these clues as your allies.

The process of learning, exploration and personal connection are all within your control. By knowing the text intimately and understanding your relationship to it, you can begin to use the audition for your own education. Empowering yourself can be critical to your confidence and self esteem. In this way you can use the system that tends to use you. Remember there is nothing more pleasurable from an auditor's standpoint than having an actor who understands and illuminates a role. It is a thrilling discovery and it is in the producer or director's best interest to hire such a person.

I wish you the best of luck!

David Esbjornson
Artistic Director, Classical Stage Company

MONOLOGUES FROM CLASSIC PLAYS

Men's Monologues

PROMETHEUS BOUND
by ÆSCHYLUS
translated by J.S. Blackie
A mountain in Scythia - Prometheus (20-30)

Chained to a mountain for stealing fire from Zeus, Prometheus
here laments his fate.

PROMETHEUS: O divine ether, and swift-
    winged winds,
And river-fountains, and of ocean waves
The multitudinous laughter, and thou
    Earth,
Boon mother of us all, and thou bright
    round
Of the all-seeing Sun, you I invoke!
Behold what ignominy of causeless wrongs
I suffer from the gods, myself a god.
  See what piercing pains shall goad
    me
  Through long ages myriad-numbered!
  With such wrongful chains hath bound
    me
  This new leader of the gods.
  Ah me! present woes and future
  I bemoan. O! when, O! when
  Shall the just redemption dawn?
Yet why thus prate? I know what ills
    await me.
No unexpected torture can surprise
My soul prophetic; and with quiet mind
We all must bear our portioned fate, nor
    idly
Court battle with a strong necessity
Alas! alas! 'tis hard to speak to the
    winds;

PROMETHEUS BOUND

Still harder to be dumb! my well-
    deservings
To mortal men are all the offence that
    bowed me
Beneath this yoke. The secret fount of
    fire
I sought, and found, and in a reed con-
    cealed it;
Whence arts have sprung to man, and life
    hath drawn
Rich store of comforts. For such deed I
    suffer
These bonds, in the broad eye of gracious
    day,
Here crucified. Ah me! ah me! who comes?
What sound, what viewless breath, thus
    taints the air,
God sent, or mortal, or of mingled kind?
What errant traveller ill-sped comes to
    view
This naked ridge of extreme Earth, and
    me?
Whoe'er thou art, a hapless god thou
    see'st
Nailed to this crag; the foe of Jove thou
    see'st.
  Him thou see'st, whom all the Immortals
  Whoso tread the Olympian threshold,
  Name with hatred; thou beholdest
  Man's best friend, and, therefore, hated
    For excess of love.
  Hark, again! I hear the whirring
  As of winged birds approaching;
  With the light strokes of their pinions

PROMETHEUS BOUND

Ether pipes ill-boding whispers!—
Alas! alas! that I should fear
Each breath that nears me.

ANTIGONE
by Sophocles
translated by Sir George Young
The royal palace at Thebes - Creon (50-60)

When Creon assumes the throne of Thebes, he addresses his generals and commands that the body of Polyneises, son of Oedipus, be left to rot in the street in defiance of the rites of the dead.

CREON: Sirs, for the ship of state—the
    Gods once more,
After much rocking on a stormy surge,
Set her on even keel. Now therefore you,
You of all others, by my summoners
I bade come hither; having found you first
Right loyal ever to the kingly power
In Laius' time; and next, while Edipus
Ordered the commonwealth; and since his
    fall,
With steadfast purposes abiding still,
Circling their progeny. Now, since they
    perished,
Both on one day, slain by a two-edged
    fate,
Striking and stricken, sullied with a stain
Of mutual fratricide, I, as you know,
In right of kinship nearest to the dead,
Possess the throne and take the supreme
    power.
Howbeit it is impossible to know
The spirit of any man, purpose or will,
Before it be displayed by exercise
In government and laws. To me, I say,
Now as of old, that pilot of the state
Who sets no hand to the best policy,

ANTIGONE

But remains tongue-tied through some
    terror, seems
Vilest of men. Him too, who sets a friend
Before his native land, I prize at nothing.
God, who seest all things always, witness
    it!
If I perceive, where safety should have
    been,
Mischief advancing, toward my citizens,
I will not sit in silence; nor account
As friend to me the country's enemy;
But thus I deem: she is our ark of safety;
And friends are made then only, when,
    embarked
Upon her deck, we ride the seas upright.
Such are the laws by which I mean to
    further
This city's welfare; and akin to these
I have given orders to the citizens
Touching the sons of Edipus. Eteocles,
Who in this city's quarrel fought and fell,
The foremost of our champions in the
    fray,
They should entomb with the full sanctity
Of rites that solemnize the downward road
Of their dead greatest. Him the while,
    his brother,
That Polynices who, returning home
A banished man, sought to lay waste with
    fire
His household Gods, his native country—
    sought
To glut himself with his own kindred's
    blood,

ANTIGONE

Or carry them away to slavery,
It has been promulgated to the city
No man shall bury, none should wail for
    him;
Unsepulchred, shamed in the eyes of
    men,
His body shall be left to be devoured
By dogs and fowls of the air. Such is my
    will.
Never with me shall wicked men usurp
The honours of the righteous; but whoe'er
Is friendly to this city shall, by me,
Living or dead, be honoured equally.

OEDIPUS REX
by Sophocles
translated by Albert Cook
The city of Thebes - Oedipus (40-60)

When Oedipus discovers that he has inadvertently killed his
father and that his wife, Queen Jocasta, is his biological mother,
he blinds himself with her brooch. Here, he explains his desire
for sightlessness.

OEDIPUS: Ah, friend,
You are my steadfast servant still,
You still remain to care for me, blind.
Alas! Alas!
You are not hid from me; I know you clearly,
And though in darkness, still I hear your voice.
[CHORUS: O dreadful doer, how did you so endure
To quench your eyes? What daimon drove you on?

(Strophe B)]

OEDIPUS: Apollo it was, Apollo, friends
Who brought it to pass these evil, evil woes of mine.
The hand of no one struck my eyes but wretched me.
For why should I see,
When nothing sweet there is to see with sight?
[CHORUS: This is just as you say.]
OEDIPUS: What more is there for me to see,
My friends, what to love,
What joy to hear a greeting?
Lead me at once away from here,
Lead me away, friends, wretched as I am,
Accursed, and hated most
Of mortal to the gods.
[CHORUS: Wretched alike in mind and in your fortune,
How I wish that I had never known you.

(Antistrophe B)]

OEDIPUS: May he perish, whoever freed me

7

OEDIPUS REX

From fierce bonds on my feet,
Snatched me from death and saved me, doing me no joy.
For if then I had died, I should not be
So great a grief to friends and to myself
[CHORUS: This also is my wish.]
OEDIPUS: I would not have come to murder my father,
Nor have been called among men
The bridegroom of her from whom I was born.
But as it is I am godless, child of unholiness,
Wretched sire in common with my father.
And if there is any evil older than evil left,
It is the lot of Oedipus.
[CHORUS: I know not how I could give you good advice,
For you would be better dead than living blind.]
OEDIPUS: That how things are was not done for the best—
Teach me not this, or give me more advice.
If I had sight, I know not with what eyes
I could ever face my father among the dead,
Or my wretched mother. What I have done to them
Is too great for a noose to expiate.
Do you think the sight of my children would be a joy
For me to see, born as they were to me?
No, never for these eyes of mine to see.
Nor the city, nor the tower, nor the sacred
Statues of gods; of these I deprive myself,
Noblest among the Thebans, born and bred,
Now suffering everything. I tell you all
To exile me as impious, shown by the gods
Untouchable and of the race of Laius.
When I uncovered such a stain on me
Could I look with steady eyes upon the people?
No, No! And if there were a way to block
The spring of hearing, I would not forbear
To lock up wholly this my wretched body.

OEDIPUS REX

I should be blind and deaf.—For it is sweet
When thought can dwell outside our evils.
Alas, Cithaeron, why did you shelter me?
Why did you not take and kill me at once, so I
Might never reveal to men whence I was born?
O Polybus, O Corinth, O my father's halls,
Ancient in fable, what an outer fairness,
A festering of evils, you raised in me.
For now I am evil found, and born of evil.
O the three paths! Alas the hidden glen,
The grove of oak, the narrow triple roads
That drank from my own hands my father's blood.
Do you remember any of the deeds
I did before you then on my way here
And what I after did? O wedlock, wedlock!
You gave me birth, and then spawned in return
Issue from the selfsame seed; you revealed
Father, brother, children, in blood relation,
The bride both wife and mother, and whatever
Actions are done most shameful among men.
But it is wrong to speak what is not good to do.
By the gods, hide me at once outside our land,
Or murder me, or hurl me in the sea
Where you shall never look on me again.
Come venture to lay your hands on this wretched man.
Do it. Be not afraid. No mortal man

(Enter CREON)

There is, except myself, to bear my evils.

THE CLOUDS
by Aristophanes
translated by T. Mitchell
Athens - Strepsiades (50-60)

The querulous old farmer finds that he cannot sleep and frets about his numerous debts.

STREPSIADES: Sleep on!
But take this with you; all these debts of
    mine
Will double on your head: a plague confound
That cursed match-maker, who drew me in
To wed, forsooth, that precious dam of
    thine.
I liv'd at ease in the country, coarsely
    clad,
Rough, free, and full withal as oil and
    honey
And store of stock could fill me, till I took,
Clown as I was, this limb of the Alcmæons,
This vain, extravagant, high-blooded
    dame:
Rare bed-fellows and dainty—were we
    not?
I, smelling of the wine-vat, figs and fleeces,
The produce of my farm, all essence she,
Saffron and harlot's kisses, paint and
    washes,
A pamper'd wanton—idle I'll not call
    her;
She took due pains in faith to work my
    ruin,
Which made me tell her, pointing to this
    cloak,
Now threadbare on my shoulders—see,

goodwife,
This is your work—in troth you toil too
    hard.   *[Boy reenters.]*
[BOY: Master, the lamp has drunk up
    all its oil.]
[STREPSIADES: Aye, 'tis a drunken lamp;
    the more fault yours;
Whelp, you shall howl for this.]
[BOY: Why? for what fault?]
[STREPSIADES: For cramming such a
    greedy wick with oil.   *[Exit boy.]*
Well! in good time this hopeful heir was
    born;
Then I and my beloved fell to wrangling
About the naming of the brat. —My wife
Would dub her colt Xanthippus or Charippus,
Or it might be Callipides, she car'd not
So 'twere equestrian the name—but I
Stuck for his grandfather Pheidonides;
At last when neither could prevail, the
    matter
Was compromis'd by calling him Pheidippides:
Then she began to fondle her sweet babe,
And taking him by th' hand—Lambkin,
    she cried
When thou art some years older thou shalt
    drive,
Megacles-like, thy chariot to the city,
Rob'd in a saffron mantle. —No, quoth I,
Not so, my boy, out thou shalt drive thy
    goats,
When thou art able, from the fields of
    Phelle,
Clad in a woollen jacket like thy father:

THE CLOUDS

But he is deaf to all these frugal rules,
And drives me on the gallop to my ruin;
Therefore all night I call my thoughts to
     council,
And after long debate find one chance
     left,
To which if I can lead him, all is safe,
If not—but soft: 'tis time that I should
     wake him.

ŚAKOONTALÁ
by Kálidása
translated by Sir Monier Monier-Williams
Ancient India - King Dushyanta (20-30)

While hunting, King Dushyanta encounters the beautiful young
Śakoontalá and is instantly smitten.

KING: *(sighing thoughtfully.)* The holy
    sage possesses magic power
In virtue of his penance; she, his ward,
Under the shadow of his tutelage,
Rests in security. I know it well;
Yet sooner shall the rushing cataract
In foaming eddies re-ascend the steep,
Than my fond heart turn back from its
    pursuit.
God of love! God of the flowery shafts!
we lovers are cruelly deceived by thee, and
by the Moon, however deserving of confidence
    you may both appear.

For not to us do these thine arrows seem
Pointed with tender flowerets; not to us
Doth the pale Moon irradiate the earth
With beams of silver fraught with cooling
    dews;
But on our fevered frames the moonbeams
    fall
Like darts of fire, and every flower tipt
    shaft
Of Káma as it probes our throbbing
    hearts;
Seems to be barbed with hardest adamant.

Adorable god of love! hast thou no

pity for me? *(In a tone of anguish.)*
How can thy arrows be so sharp when
they are pointed with flowers? Ah! I
know the reason:
E'en now in thine unbodied essence lurks
The fire of Siva's anger, like the flame
That ever hidden in the secret depths
Of ocean smoulders there unseen. How
    else
Could'st thou, all immaterial as thou art,
Inflame our hearts thus fiercely?—thou,
    whose form
Was scorched to ashes by a sudden flash
From the offended god's terrific eye.
    Yet methinks,
Welcome this anguish, welcome to my
    heart
These rankling wounds inflicted by the
    god,
Who on his scutcheon bears the monster-
    fish
Slain by his prowess; welcome death it-
    self,
So that, commissioned by the lord of
    love,
This fair one be my executioner.
    Adorable divinity! Can I by no re-
proaches excite your commiseration?
Have I not daily offered at thy shrine
Innumerable vows, the only food
Of thine ethereal essence? Are my prayers
Thus to be slighted? Is it meet that thou
Should'st aim thy shafts at thy true
    votary's heart,

ŚAKOONTALÁ

Drawing thy bow-string even to thy ear?
*(Pacing up and down in a melancholy
manner.)* Now that the holy men have
completed their rites, and have no more
need of my services, how shall I dispel
my melancholy? *(Sighing.)* I have but
one resource. Oh for another sight of
the idol of my soul! I will seek her.
(Glancing at the sun.) In all probability,
as the sun's heat is now at its height,
Śakoontalá is passing her time under the
shade of the bowers on the banks of the
Máliní, attended by her maidens. I will
go and look for her there. *(Walking and
looking about.)* I suspect the fair one
has but just passed by this avenue of
young trees.

Here, as she tripped along, her fingers
    plucked
The opening buds; these lacerated plants,
Shorn of their fairest blossoms by her
    hand,
Seem like dismembered trunks, whose
    recent wounds
Are still unclosed; while from the bleed-
    ing socket
Of many a severed stalk, the milky juice
Still slowly trickles, and betrays her path.

(Feeling a breeze.)

    What a delicious breeze meets me in
this spot!
Here may the zephyr, fragrant with the
scent

ŚAKOONTALÁ

Of lotuses, and laden with the spray
Caught from the waters of the rippling
 stream,
Fold in its close embrace my fevered
 limbs.
(Walking and looking about.) She must
be somewhere in the neighbourhood of this
arbour of overhanging creepers enclosed
by plantations of cane; *(Looking down.)*
For at the entrance here I plainly see
A line of footsteps printed in the sand.
Here are the fresh impressions of her
 feet;
Their well-known outline faintly marked
 in front,
More deeply towards the heel; betokening
The graceful undulation of her gait.
I will peep through those branches.
(Walking and looking. With transport.)
Ah! now my eyes are gratified by an
entrancing sight. Yonder is the beloved
of my heart reclining on a rock strewn
with flowers, and attended by her two
friends. How fortunate! Concealed behind the leaves, I will listen to their
conversation, without raising their suspicions.

ADAM
The Mystery of Adam
by Anonymous
translated from the French and Latin by Edward Noble Stone
The Garden of Eden - Adam (20's)

After surrendering to temptation, Adam here rages at Eve for having defied God.

ADAM: O! sinful wretch! What have
   I done?
Now my avoidless death's begun!
Now, without rescue, am I dead;
My fortune fair is evil sped;
My lot, a little time ago
So happy, now is turned to woe;
I my Creator did forsake
Through counsel of my evil make.
O! sinner lost! What shall I do?
How can I now my Maker view?
Upon my Maker can I look,
Whom through my folly I forsook?
Ne'er such ill bargain did I strike!
Now do I know what sin is like!
O Death! Why dost thou let me live,
Nor to the earth clean riddance give?
Why, cumbering earth, do I yet stay?
The depths of hell must I essay;
In hell my dwelling aye shall be
Until one come to succour me.
In hell henceforward I shall fare,
And whence shall help come to me there?
Whence shall aid thither come to me?
Who from such pains shall set me free?
Why did I thus my Lord offend?
Now there is none can be my friend;

ADAM

None will there be can me avail;
Lost am I now, withouten fail!
Against my Lord I've done such sin,
No suit with him can I begin,
For right is he, and wrong am I.
O God! 'Neath what a curse I lie!
Who, henceforth, will take thought of me,
Who've wronged the King of Majesty?
'Gainst Heaven's own king such wrong
    I've done
That claim upon him have I none.
No friend I have, no neighbour near,
Who as my surety might appear;
And whom shall I beseech for aid,
When mine own wife hath me betrayed,
Whom God gave me my fere to be?
An evil counsel gave she me!
Alas! O Eve!

(Then shall he look upon
Eve, his wife, and shall say:)

Insensate wife!
In an ill hour I gave thee life!
O had that rib been burned, alas!
That brought me to this evil pass!
Had but the fire that rib consumed,
That me to such confusion doomed!
Why, when from me the rib he drew,
Burned he it not, nor me then slew?
The rib the body hath betrayed,
Ill-treated, and all useless made.
I know not what to say or try;
Unless grace reach me from on high,
From pain I cannot be released,
Such malady on me hath seized.
Alas! O Eve! Woe worth the day—

18

ADAM

Such torment holdeth me in sway—
Thou e'er becamest wife to me!
Now I am lost through heeding thee;
Through heeding thee I'm in this plight,
Brought down most low from a great
    height.
Thence will no mortal rescue me—
None, save the God of majesty.
What say I? Wretch! Why named I
    him?
He help? I've gained his anger grim!
None will e'er bring me succour—none
Save him who'll come as Mary's son.
From none can I henceforth get aid
Since we our trust with God betrayed.
Then, let all be as God ordains;
No course, except to die, remains.

THE SUMMONING OF EVERYMAN
by Anonymous
Heaven - God

After lamenting the state of humankind, God summons Death and instructs this entity to bring his message to Everyman.

GOD: I perceive here in my majesty
How that all creatures be to me unkind,
Living without dread in worldly prosperity.
Of ghostly sight the people be so blind;
Drowned in sin, they know me not for their God.
In worldly riches is all their mind.
They fear not my righteousness, that sharp rod.
My law that I showed when I for them died
They forget clean, and shedding of my blood so red.
I hanged between two thieves, it cannot be denied;
To get them life, I suffered to be dead.
I healed their feet; with thorns hurt was my head.
I could do no more than I did truly.
And now I see the people do clean forsake me;
They use the seven deadly sins damnable,
As pride, covetousness, wrath, and lechery
Now in the world be made commendale.
And thus they leave of angels the heavenly company.
Everyman liveth so after his own pleasure,
And yet of their life they be not sure.
I see the more that I them forbear,
The worse they are from year to year.
All that liveth appeareth fast;
Therefore I will in all the haste
Have a reckoning of everyman's person.
For and I leave the people thus alone
In their life and wicked tempests,
Verily they will become much worse than beasts.
For now one would by envy another up eat;

20

THE SUMMONING OF EVERYMAN

Charity they all do clean forget.
I hoped well that everyman
In my glory should make his mansion,
And thereto I had them all elect;
But now I see, like traitors deject,
They thank me not for the pleasure that I do them meant
Nor yet for their being that I them have lent.
I proffered the people great multitude of mercy,
And few there be that asketh it heartily.
They be so cumbered with wordly riches,
That needs on them I must do justice—
On everyman living without fear.

BILORA

by Angelo Beolco, called Il Ruzzante
translated by Babette and Glenn Hughes
Medieval Venice - Andronico (30-50)

Here, the bored Andronico ruminates on his latest acquisition:
another man's wife.

ANDRONICO: *(Soliloquizing.)* Well, there's no doubt about it: if
you don't do childish things when you are young, you're sure to
want to do them when you're old. It reminds me of the time that
Messires Nikolas d'Allegri and Panthasilus of the house of
Bucentaure, heaven bless their memory, admonished me. Their
Excellencies said to me: "What's the use, Andronico, of this
melancholy mood in which you seem to take such delight? What the
devil! Go and find yourself a girl and enjoy yourself with her.
When do you expect to enjoy life—when you're no longer able to?
You seem to us a most unnatural man, a strange man, a man
bewitched. But take note and remember that in your old age you
will commit some folly for the sake of love." And that is just what
has happened. As a matter of fact I would almost rather be amorous
now than to have been so in my youth were it not that a certain thing
thwarts my desires: that is, knowing that *non respondent ultima
primis.* Ah, the devil! It is a miserable business, this growing old!
tamen it is not that I lack courage. But enough! Let us say no more
about it, for after all I am not decrepit. Love works wonders. Look
at the way I have stolen this girl from her husband. I have risked
my life in order to possess her—so deeply am I in love, and so fond
of her. And then *breviter concludendo,* she is a very angel of a girl,
a cherubim, with a mouth that begs to be kissed. Altogether I fear
only one thing, and that troubles me a good deal, the fear that
someone will come to take her away from me. Ah, but such a one
will be unwelcome, for I have decided to continue my pleasure, and
never again be without it. If she does her duty by me, I will never
be stingy with her, so she will always be happy. Already I have
signed over securities to her, leaving her free to control my property

BILORA

as she likes, and to spend her leisure time in the house or outside of it, without consulting me or giving an account to anyone. It's a very fine thing for her, being a lady and a mistress. She rules everything, big and little. And all she has to do is give commands. Being satisfied, she will know how to treat me properly. But ah! what would I not give if she would only condescend to stir the very depths of my soul! But there—let us go up and pay her a little visit. She puts me in such a fine humor; she fondles me so! If I couldn't play with her I'd lose my head completely and neglect my business. I swear I feel so light on my feet I could lance the four figures of Badin, and after that the *Strapassao,* the *Rosina,* and in fact the whole bouquet of flower-figures. And that would be no small accomplishment. Ah yes, she will prove useful to me in a thousand ways, this girl: she will take care of me when I suffer from catarrh, and when I am bored; she will be a comfort to me when I want to talk over my business affairs.

BILORA
by Angelo Beolco, called Il Ruzzante
translated by Babette and Glenn Hughes
Medieval Venice - Bilora (30-40)

Bilora, a simple peasant, here plans to murder the man who has stolen his wife.

BILORA: *(Alone.)* By the blood of a limping bitch, but all my schemes have gone topsy-turvy, and I am flat on my back. Ah, yes! It's enough to make him split his breeches laughing. Never mind! The question is, what am I going to do about it? My life is ruined. It is best that I pick up my feet and get away from here. One thing is sure: I'll never be in danger of feeling bored so long as I'm so mad. Meanwhile I know exactly what I'm going to do. When I see him leave the house I'll jump on him all of a sudden and knock him off his legs. He will hit the ground at the first whack. Then I'll beat him up and down and across, and it will be a wonder if I don't scratch out his eyes and kill him. By God, yes, it will be too bad if I can't bully him into letting her go. Besides that, I'll talk to him in the language of a Spanish soldier; he will think there are at least eight men surrounding him. I had better practice a little the way I am going about it. First I will draw my knife. Let's see if it shines. Damned if it's very bright. He won't get much of a scare out of it. Now let's suppose, *verbo gratia,* that he is walking along over there, and that here am I, Bilora, who knows how to get what he wants. First I will commence to blaspheme and to swear by all the Christeleison of Padua, the Virgin Mary and the Dominustecum. A curse on you, son of a dog! Jew, go hang yourself. I know just how to kick the life out of your buttocks, and jerk you and maul you within an inch of death. Then I'll pull him out of his cloak, put it on my own back, undress him from head to foot, and then run away as fast as my legs will carry me, leaving him spread out on the ground like a big piece of filth. After that I will sell his cloak, buy myself a horse, and join the army. After all, I have no desire to go back home. Ah, yes! I know how to handle things! I wish he would show up, and not be so slow about leaving the house. Hush! Is that him coming now? Has he passed the door? Yes! May the worms eat you, old carcass! Suffering Christ, where is he then? No, he hasn't left the house yet. I'm lucky. Maybe he won't come out again at all. Hush! I swear I hear him coming. Yes, here he comes! I won't budge from this spot. Heaven keep me from jumping on him before he closes the door!

THE TRAGICAL HISTORY OF DR. FAUSTUS
by Christopher Marlowe
Dr. Faustus' study - Dr. Faustus (30-50)

Here, we encounter the doctor in his study. As he pours over his collection of ancient texts, he reveals his desire for forbidden knowledge.

FAUSTUS: Settle thy studies, Faustus,
    and begin
To sound the depth of that thou wilt
    profess:
Having commenc'd, be a divine in show,
Yet level at the end of every art,
And live and die in Aristotle's works.
Sweet Analytics, 'tis thou hast ravish'd
    me!
Bene disserere est finis logices.
Is, to dispute well, logic's chiefest end?
Affords this art no greater miracle?
Then read no more; thou hast attain'd
    that end:
A greater subject fitteth Faustus' wit:
Bid Economy farewell, and Galen come,
Seeing, *Ubi desinit philosophus, ibi incipit
    medicus:*
Be a physician, Faustus; heap up gold,
And be eternis'd for some wondrous cure
Summum bonum medicinæ sanitas,
The end of physic is our body's health.
Why, Faustus, hast thou not attain'd that
    end?
Is not thy common talk found aphorisms?
Are not thy bills hung up as monuments,
Whereby whole cities have escap'd the
    plague,

And thousand desperate maladies been
    eas'd?
Yet art thou still but Faustus, and a man.
Couldst thou make men to live eternally,
Or, being dead, raise them to life again,
Then this profession were to be esteem'd.
Physic, farewell! Where is Justinian?

(Reads.)

Si una eademque res legatur duobus, alter
    rem, alter valorem, rei, etc.
A pretty case of paltry legacies!   *(Reads.)*
Exhæreditare filium non potest pater nisi,
    etc.
Such is the subject of the institute,
And universal body of the law:
This study fits a mercenary drudge,
Who aims at nothing but external trash;
Too servile and illiberal for me.
When all is done, divinity is best:
Jerome's Bible, Faustus; view it well.

(Reads.)

Stipendium peccati mors est. Ha! *Stipendium,*
    etc.
The reward of sin is death: that's hard.

(Reads.)

Si peccasse negamus, fallimur, et nulia
    est in nobis veritas;
If we say that we have no sin, we deceive
    ourselves, and there's no truth in
    us.
Why, then, belike we must sin, and so
    consequently die:
Ay, we must die an everlasting death.
What doctrine call you this, *Che sera,*
    sera,

THE TRAGICAL HISTORY OF DR. FAUSTUS

What will be, shall be? Divinity, adieu!
These metaphysics of magicians,
And necromantic books are heavenly;
Lines, circles, scenes, letters, and characters;
Ay, these are those that Faustus most
    desires.
O, what a world of profit and delight,
Of power, of honour, of omnipotence,
Is promis'd to the studious artisan!
All things that move between the quiet
    poles
Shall be at my command: emperors and
    kings
Are but obeyed in their several provinces,
Nor can they raise the wind, or rend the
    clouds;
But his dominion that exceeds in this,
Stretcheth as far as doth the mind of
    man;
A sound magician is a mighty god:
Here, Faustus, tire thy brains to gain
    a deity.

THE TRAGICAL HISTORY OF DR. FAUSTUS
by Christopher Marlowe
Dr. Faustus' study - Faustus (30-50)

Having sold his soul to the Devil in return for knowledge of black magic, Faustus now faces his damnation. Realizing his soul is lost, he despairs and repents before God.

FAUSTUS: Ah, Faustus.
Now hast thou but one bare hour to live,
And then thou must be damn'd perpetually!
Stand still, you ever-moving spheres of
    heaven,
That time may cease, and midnight never
    come;
Fair Nature's eye, rise, rise again, and
    make
Perpetual day; or let this hour be but
A year, a month, a week, a natural day,
That Faustus may repent and save his
    soul!
O lente, lente currite, noctis equi!
The stars move still, time runs, the clock
    will strike,
The devil will come, and Faustus must be
    damn'd.
O, I'll leap up to my God!—Who pulls me
    down?—
See, see, where Christ's blood streams in
    the firmament!
One drop would save my soul, half a drop:
    ah, my Christ!—
Ah, rend not my heart for naming of my
    Christ!
Yet will I call on him: O, spare me,
    Lucifer!—

THE TRAGICAL HISTORY OF DR. FAUSTUS

Where is it now? 'tis gone: and see,
    where God
Stretcheth out his arm, and bends his
    ireful brows!
Mountains and hills, come, come, and fall
    on me,
And hide me from the heavy wrath of
    God!
No, no!
Then will I headlong run into the earth:
Earth, gape! O, no, it will not harbour
    me!
You stars that reign'd at my nativity,
Whose influence hath allotted death and
    hell,
Now draw up Faustus, like a foggy mist,
Into the entrails of yon labouring clouds,
That, when you vomit forth into the
    air,
My limbs may issue from your smoky
    mouths,
So that my soul may but ascend to
    heaven!

(The clock strikes the half-hour.)

Ah, half the hour is past! 'twill all be
    past anon.
O God,
If thou wilt not have mercy on my soul,
Yet for Christ's sake, whose blood hath
    ransom'd me,
Impose some end to my incessant pain;
Let Faustus live in hell a thousand years,
A hundred thousand, and at last be sav'd!
O, no end is limited to damned souls!

THE TRAGICAL HISTORY OF DR. FAUSTUS

Why wert thou not a creature wanting
    soul?
Or why is this immortal that thou hast?
Ah, Pythagoras' metempsychosis, were
    that true,
This soul should fly from me, and I be
    chang'd
Unto some brutish beast! all beasts are
    happy,
For when they die,
Their souls are soon dissolv'd in elements;
But mine must live still to be plagu'd in
    hell.
Curs'd be the parents that engender'd me!
No, Faustus, curse thyself, curse Lucifer
That hath depriv'd thee of the joys of
    heaven.

(The clock strikes twelve.)

O, it strikes, it strikes! Now, body, turn
    to air,
Or Lucifer will bear thee quick to hell!

(Thunder and lightning.)

O soul, be chang'd into little water-drops,
And fall into the ocean, ne'er be found!

(Enter DEVILS.)

My God, my God, look not so fierce on
    me!
Adders and serpents, let me breathe a
    while!
Ugly hell, gape not! come not, Lucifer!
I'll burn my books!—Ah, Mephistophilis!

TAMBURLAINE THE GREAT
by Christopher Marlowe
Medieval Persia - Tamburlaine (30-40)

Following a successful military rout of Turkey, the bloodthirsty
Tamburlaine takes a moment to gloat over his captives.

TAMBURLAINE: Now clear the triple region of the air,
And let the majesty of Heaven behold
Their scourge and terror tread on emperors.
Smile stars, that reign'd at my nativity,
And dim the brightness of their neighbour lamps!
Disdain to borrow light of Cynthia!
For I, the chiefest lamp of all the earth,
First rising in the East with mild aspect,
But fixed now in the meridian line,
Will send up fire to your turning spheres,
And cause the sun to borrow light of you.
My sword struck fire from his coat of steel,
Even in Bithynia, when I took this Turk;
As when a fiery exhalation,
Wrapp'd in the bowels of a freezing cloud,
Fighting for passage, makes the welkin crack,
And casts a flash of lightning to the earth:
But ere I march to wealthy Persia,
Or leave Damascus and th' Egyptian fields,
As was the fame of Clymen's brain-sick son,
That almost brent the axle-tree of Heaven,
So shall our swords, our lances, and our shot
Fill all the air with fiery meteors.
Then, when the sky shall wax as red as blood,
It shall be said I made it red myself
To make me think of naught but blood and war.

TAMBURLAINE THE GREAT
by Christopher Marlowe
Medieval Persia - Tamburlaine (30-40)

The conqueror of Turkey and Persia is smitten by the beautiful Zenocrate. Here, the shameless butcher is surprised by his feelings.

TAMBURLAINE: A sight as baneful to their souls, I think,
As are Thessalian drugs or mithridate:
But go, my lords, put the rest to the sword.

[Exeunt (all except Tamburlaine.)]

Ah, fair Zenocrate! divine Zenocrate!
Fair is too foul an epithet for thee,
That in thy passion for thy country's love,
And fear to see thy kingly father's harm,
With hair dishevell'd wip'st thy watery cheeks;
And, like to Flora in her morning's pride
Shaking her silver tresses in the air,
Rain'st on the earth resolved pearl in showers,
And sprinklest sapphires on thy shining face,
Where Beauty, mother to the Muses, sits
And comments volumes with her ivory pen,
Taking instructions from thy flowing eyes;
Eyes when that Ebena steps to Heaven,
In silence of thy solemn evening's walk,
Making the mantle of the richest night,
The moon, the planets, and the meteors, light.
There angels in their crystal armours fight
A doubtful battle with my tempted thoughts
For Egypt's freedom, and the Soldan's life;
His life that so consumes Zenocrate,
Whose sorrows lay more siege unto my soul,
Than all my army to Damascus' walls:
And neither Persia's sovereign, nor the Turk
Troubled my senses with conceit of foil

TAMBURLAINE THE GREAT

So much by much as doth Zenocrate.
What is beauty, saith my sufferings, then?
If all the pens that ever poets held
Had fed the feeling of their masters' thoughts,
And every sweetness that inspir'd their hearts,
Their minds, and muses on admired themes;
If all the heavenly quintessence they still
From their immortal flowers of poesy,
Wherein, as in a mirror, we perceive
The highest reaches of a human wit:
If these had made one poem's period,
And all combin'd in beauty's worthiness,
Yet should there hover in their restless heads
One thought, one grace, one wonder, at the least,
Which into words no virtue can digest.
But how unseemly is it for my sex,
My discipline of arms and chivalry,
My nature, and the terror of my name,
To harbour thoughts effeminate and faint!
Save only that in beauty's just applause,
With whose instinct the soul of man is touch'd;—
And every warrior that is rapt with love
Of fame, of valour, and of victory,
Must needs have beauty beat on his conceits:
I thus conceiving and subduing both
That which hath stoop'd the tempest of the gods,
Even from the fiery-spangled veil of Heaven,
To feel the lovely warmth of shepherds' flames,
And mask in cottages of strowed weeds,
Shall give the world to note, for all my birth,
That virtue solely is the sum of glory,
And fashions men with true nobility.

THE TAMING OF THE SHREW
by William Shakespeare
edited by Robert B. Heilman
Medieval Padua - Petruchio (30's)

Here, the stouthearted Petruchio divulges his plan to conquer his headstrong wife with kindness.

PETRUCHIO: Thus have I politicly begun my reign,
And 'tis my hope to end successfully.
My falcon now is sharp and passing empty,
And till she stoop she must not be full gorged,
For then she never looks upon her lure.
Another way I have to man my haggard,
To make her come and know her keeper's call,
That is, to watch her as we watch these kites
That bate and beat and will not be obedient.
She eat no meat today, nor none shall eat.
Last night she slept not, nor tonight she shall not.
As with the meat, some undeserv'd fault
I'll find about the making of the bed,
And here I'll fling the pillow, there the bolster,
This way the coverlet, another way the sheets.
Ay, and amid this hurly I intend
That all is done in reverent care of her,
And in conclusion she shall watch all night.
And if she chance to nod I'll rait and brawl
And with the clamor keep her still awake.
This is a way to kill a wife with kindness,
And thus I'll curb her mad and headstrong humor.
He that knows better how to tame a shrew,
Now let him speak—'tis charity to show.

A MIDSUMMER NIGHT'S DREAM
by William Shakespeare
edited by Wolfgang Clemen
An enchanted forest - Puck (15-20)

Puck here reports to his master, Oberon, of Titania's love for an ass.

PUCK: My mistress with a monster is in love.
Near to her close and consecrated bower,
While she was in her dull and sleeping hour,
A crew of patches, rude mechanicals,
That work for bread upon Athenian stalls,
Were met together to rehearse a play,
Intended for great Theseus' nuptial day.
The shallowest thickskin of that barren sort,
Who Pyramus presented in their sport,
Forsook his scene, and entered in a brake.
When I did him at this advantage take,
An ass's nole I fix'd on his head.
Anon his Thisby must be answer'd,
And forth my mimic comes. When they him spy,
As wild geese that the creeping fowler eye,
Or russet-pated choughs, many in sort,
Rising and cawing at the gun's report,
Sever themselves and madly sweep the sky,
So, at his sight, away his fellows fly;
And, at our stamp, here o'er and o'er one falls;
He murder cries, and help from Athens calls.
Their sense thus weak, lost with their fears thus
    strong,
Made senseless things begin to do them wrong;
For briers and thorns at their apparel snatch;
Some sleeves, some hats, from yielders all things
    catch.
I led them on in this distracted fear,

A MIDSUMMER NIGHT'S DREAM

And left sweet Pyramus translated there:
When in that moment, so it came to pass,
Titania waked, and straightway loved an ass.

THE MALCONTENT
by John Marston
The Duke's court in Genoa - Mendoza (20-30)

Here, the minion of the Duchess waxes with eloquent enthusiasm
on the benefits of being favored in the court.

MENDOZA: Now good Elysium, what a delicious heaven is it for
a man to be in a prince's favour: O sweet God, O pleasure! O
Fortune! O all thou best of life! what should I think, what say, what
do, to be a favourite, a minion? to have a general timorous respect
observe a man, a stateful silence in his presence: solitariness in his
absence, a confused hum and busy murmur of obsequious suitors
training him; the cloth held up, and way proclaimed before him:
petitionary vassals licking the pavement with their slavish knees,
whilst some odd palace lampreels that engender with snakes, and are
full of eyes on both sides, with a kind of insinuated humbleness fix
all their delights upon his brow: O blessed state, what a ravishing
prospect doth the Olympus of favour yield! Death, I cornute the
Duke. Sweet women, most sweet ladies, nay angels; by heaven, he
is more accursed than a devil that hates you, or is hated by you, and
happier than a God that loves you, or is beloved by you; you
preservers of mankind, life-blood of society, who would live, nay,
who can live without you? O Paradise, how majestical is your
austerer presence! how imperiously chaste is your more modest face!
but O! how full of ravishing attraction is your pretty, petulant,
languishing, lasciviously-composed countenance: those amorous
smiles, those soul-warming sparkling glances, ardent as those flames
that sing'd the world by heedless Phaëton! in body how delicate, in
soul how witty, in discourse how pregnant, in life how wary, in
favours how judicious, in day how sociable, and in night how—O
pleasure unutterable! Indeed it is most certain, one man cannot
deserve only to enjoy a beauteous woman: but a duchess! In despite
of Phoebus I'll write a sonnet instantly in praise of her.

When the Duke and his men ask Othello how he was able to win the fair Desdemona, he offers the following explanation.

OTHELLO: I do beseech you,
Send for the lady to the Sagittary,
And let her speak of me before her father.
If you do find me foul in her report,
The trust, the office, I do hold of you,
Not only take away, but let your sentence
Even fall upon my life.
[DUKE: *(To attending officers.)* Fetch Desdemona hither.]
OTHELLO: Ancient, conduct them, you best know the place.
(IAGO exits with attendants.)
And till she come, as truly as to heaven
I do confess the vices of my blood,
So justify to your grave ears I'll present
How I did thrive in this fair lady's love,
And she in mine.
[DUKE: Say it, Othello.]
OTHELLO: Her father loved me, oft invited me,
Still questioned me the story of my life,
From year to year, the battles, sieges, fortunes,
That I have passed.
I ran it through, even from my boyish days,
To the very moment that he bade me tell it.
Wherein I spoke of most disastrous chances,
Of moving accidents, by flood and field;
Of hair-breadth 'scapes i' the imminent deadly breach;
Of being taken by the insolent foe,
And sold to slavery; of my redemption thence,
And portance in my travel's history;

OTHELLO

Wherein of antars vast, and deserts wild,
Rough quarries, rocks, and hills whose heads touch heaven,
It was my hint to speak—such was the process;
And of the cannibals that each other eat,
The Anthropophagi, and men whose heads
Do grow beneath their shoulders. These things to hear,
Would Desdemona seriously incline;
But still the house affairs would draw her thence;
Which ever as she could with haste dispatch,
She'd come again, and with a greedy ear,
Devour up my discourse; which I, observing,
Took once a pliant hour, and found good means
To draw from her a prayer of earnest heart,
That I would all my pilgrimage dilate,
Whereof by parcels she had something heard,
But not intentively. I did consent;
And often did beguile her of her tears,
When I did speak of some distressful stroke,
That my youth suffered. My story being done,
She gave me for my pains a world of sighs;
She swore in faith, 'twas strange, 'twas passing strange;
'Twas pitiful, 'twas wondrous pitiful;
She wished she had not heard it; yet she wished
That heaven had made her such a man; she thanked me,
And bade me, if I had a friend that loved her,
I should but teach him how to tell my story,
And that would woo her. Upon this hint I spake:
She loved me for the dangers I had passed;
And I loved her that she did pity them.
This only is the witchcraft I have used.
Here comes the lady; let her witness it.

THE REVENGER'S TRAGEDY
attributed to Cyril Touneur
17th Century Europe - Vindice (20-30)

When the woman he loves is poisoned by the Duke for refusing his advances, Vindice allows himself to become filled with hatred.

VINDICE: Duke: royal lecher; go, grey-hair'd adultery,
And thou his son, as impious steept as he:
And thou his bastard true-begot in evil:
And thou his Duchess that will do with Devil,
Four ex'lent characters—O that marrowless age
Would stuff the hollow bones with damn'd desires,
And 'stead of heat kindle infernal fires,
Within the spend-thrift veins of a dry Duke,
A parcht and juiceless luxur. O God! one
That has scarce blood enough to live upon,
And he to riot it like a son and heir?
O the thought of that
Turns my abused heart-strings into fret.
Thou sallow picture of my poisoned love,
My study's ornament, thou shell of death,
Once the bright face of my betrothed lady,
When life and beauty naturally fill'd out
These ragged imperfections;
When two heaven-pointed diamonds were set
In those unsightly rings;—then 'twas a face
So far beyond the artificial shine
Of any woman's bought complexion
That the uprightest man, (if such there be,
That sin but seven times a day) broke custom
And made up eight with looking after her.
Oh she was able to ha' made a usurer's son
Melt all his patrimony in a kiss,
And what his father fifty years told

THE REVENGER'S TRAGEDY

To have consum'd, and yet his suit been cold:
But oh accursed palace!
Thee when thou wert apparell'd in thy flesh,
The old Duke poison'd,
Because thy purer part would not consent
Unto his palsy-lust, for old men lust-full
Do show like young men angry, eager-violent,
Out-bid like their limited performances—
O 'ware an old man hot and vicious:
'Age as in gold, in lust is covetous.'
Vengeance, thou murder's quit-rent, and whereby
Thou show'st thyself tenant to tragedy,
Oh keep thy day, hour, minute, I beseech,
For those thou hast determin'd: hum: whoe'er knew
Murder unpaid? faith, give revenge her due
Sh'as kept touch hitherto—be merry, merry,
Advance thee, O thou terror to fat folks,
To have their costly three-pil'd flesh worn off
As bare as this—for banquets, ease and laughter
Can make great men, as greatness goes by clay,
But wise men little are more great than they.

A man made bitter by the fact of his illegitimate birth here vows
revenge upon his father.

SPURIO: Duke, thou didst do me wrong, and by thy act
Adultry is my nature;
Faith if the truth were known, I was begot
After some gluttonous dinner, some stirring dish
Was my first father; when deep healths went round,
And ladies' cheeks were painted red with wine,
Their tongues as short and nimble as their heels
Uttering words sweet and thick; and when they rose,
Were merrily dispos'd to fall again,
In such a whisp'ring and withdrawing hour,
When base male-bawds kept sentinel at stair-head,
Was I stol'n softly; oh—damnation met
The sin of feasts, drunken adultery.
I feel it swell me; my revenge is just,
I was begot in impudent wine and lust:
Step-mother I consent to thy desires,
I love thy mischief well, but I hate thee,
And those three cubs thy sons, wishing confusion
Death and disgrace may be their epitaphs;
As for my brother the Duke's only son,
Whose birth is more beholding to report
Than mine, and yet perhaps as falsely sown
(Women must not be trusted with their own),
I'll loose my days upon him, hate all I,
Duke, on thy brow I'll draw my bastardy.
For indeed a bastard by nature should make cuckolds,
    because he is the son of a cuckold-maker.

THE KNIGHT OF THE BURNING PESTLE
by Beaumont and Fletcher

London, Watham Forest and Moldavia - Ralph (20-30)
> When his master writes a play, this simple grocer's assistant
> finds himself having to portray the May Lord.

RALPH: London, to thee I do present the merry month of May;
La each true subject be content to hear me what I say:
For from the top of conduit-head, as plainly may appear.
I will both tell my name to you, and wherefore I came here.
My name is Ralph, by due descent though not ignoble I,
Ya far inferior to the flock of gracious grocery;
And by the common counsel of my fellows in the Strand,
W'th gilded staff and crossed scarf, the May-lord here I stand.
Rejoice, oh, English hearts, rejoice! rejoice, oh, lovers dear!
Rejoice, oh, city, town, and country! rejoice, eke every Shire!
For now the fragrant flowers do spring and sprout in seemly sort,
The little birds do sit and sing, the lambs do make pule sport;
And now the birchen-tree doth bud, that makes the schoolboy cry;
The morris rings, while hobby-horse doth foot it feateously;
The lords and ladies now abroad, for their disport and play,
Do kiss sometimes upon the grass, and sometimes in the hay;
Now butter with a leaf of sage is good to purge the blood;
Fly Venus and phlebotomy, for they are neither good.
Now litte fish on tender stone begin to cast their bellies,
And sluggish snails, that erst were mew'd. do creep out of their
    shellies;
The rumbling rivers now do warm, for little boys to paddle;
The sturdy steed now goes to grass, and up they hang his saddle;
The heavy han, the bellowing buck, the rascal, and the pricket,
Are now among the yeoman's peas, and leave the fearful thicket:
And be like them, oh, you, I say, of this same noble town.
And lip alop your velvet heads, and slipping offyour gown,
With bells on legs, and napkins clean unto your shoulders tied,
With scarfs and ganers as you please, and "Hey for our town!"
    cried,

THE KNIGHT OF THE BURNING PESTLE

March out, and show your willing minds, by twenty and by twenty,
To Hogsden or to Newington, where ale and cakes are plenty;
And let it ne 'er be said for shame, that we the youths of London
Lay thrumming of our caps at home, and left our custom undone.
Up, then, I say, both young and old, both man and maid amaying,
With drums, and guns that bounce aloud, and merry tabor playing!
Which to prolong, God save our king, and send his country peace,
And root out treason from the land! and so, my friends, I cease.

THE KNIGHT OF THE BURNING PESTLE
by Beaumont and Fletcher
London, Watham Forest, and Moldavia - Jasper (20-30)

When he is wronged by the merchant to whom he had been apprenticed, Jasper feigns his own death so that he can appear to his tormentor as a "ghost" and punish him.

JASPER: Forbear thy pains, fond man! it is too late.
[VENTUREWELL: Heaven bless me! Jasper!]
JASPER: Ay, I am his ghost,
Whom thou hast injur'd for his constant love,
Fond worldly wretch! who dost not understand
In death that true hearts cannot parted be.
First know, thy daughter is quite borne away
On wings of angels, through the liquid air,
To far out of thy reach, and never more
Shalt thou behold her face: but she and I
Will in another world enjoy our loves;
Where neither father's anger, poverty,
Nor any cross that troubles earthly men,
Shall make us sever our united hearts.
And never shalt thou sit or be alone
In any place, but I will visit thee
With ghastly looks, and put into thy mind
The great offences which thou didst to me.
When thou art at thy table with thy friends,
Merry in heart, and fill'd with swelling wine,
I'll come in midst of all thy pride and mirth,
Invisible to all men but thyself,
And whisper such a sad tale in thine ear
Shall make thee let the cup fall from thy hand,
And stand as mute and pale as death itself.

EPICOENE
or The Silent Woman
by Benjamin Johnson
17th Century London - Morose (30-40)

Morose, a man who craves silence, here lectures his servant on
the most effective way to communicate without speaking.

MOROSE: Cannot I, yet, find out a more compendious method,
than by this trunk, to save my servants the labour of speech, and
mine ears the discord of sounds? Let me see: all discourses but
mine own afflict me; they seem harsh, impertinent, and irksome. Is
it not possible, that thou should'st answer me by signs, and I
apprehend thee, fellow? Speak not, though I question you. You
have taken the ring off from the street door, as I bade you? Answer
me not by speech, but by silence; unless it be otherwise *(Mute
makes a leg.)* —Very good. And you have fastened on a thick quilt,
or flock-bed, on the outside of the door; that if they knock with their
daggers, or with brick-bats, they can make no noise?—But with your
leg, your answer, unless it be otherwise *(makes a leg.)* —Very
good. This is not only fit modesty in a servant, but good state and
discretion in a master. And you have been with Cutbeard the
barber, to have him come to me? *(makes a leg.)* —Good. And, he
will come presently? Answer me not but with your leg, unless it be
otherwise; if it be otherwise, shake your head, or shrug *[makes a
leg.)* —So! Your Italian and Spaniard are wise in these: and it is a
frugal and comely gravity. How long will it be ere Cutbeard come?
Stay; if an hour, hold up your whole hand, if half an hour, two
fingers; if a quarter, one; *(holds up a finger bent.)* —Good: half a
quarter? 'tis well. And have you given him a key, to come in without knocking? *(makes a leg.)* —Good. And is the lock oil'd, and
the hinges, to-day? *(makes a leg.)* —Good. And the quilting of the
stairs nowhere worn out and bare? *(makes a leg.)* —Very good.
I see, by much doctrine, and impulsion, it may be effected; stand by.
The Turk, in this divine discipline, is admirable, exceeding all the
potentates of the earth; still waited on by mutes; and all his

47

commands so executed; yea, even in the war, as I have heard, and in his marches, most of his charges and directions given by signs, and with silence: an exquisite art! and I am heartily asham'd, and angry oftentimes, that the princes of Christendom should suffer a barbarian to transcend 'em in so high a point of felicity. I will practise it hereafter. *(One winds a horn without.)* —How now? oh! oh! what villain, what prodigy of mankind is that? look. *(Exit Mute. Again.)* —Oh! cut his throat, cut his throat! what murderer, hell-hound, devil can this be?

THE ATHEIST'S TRAGEDY
by Cyril Tourneur
A 16th century French baronial estate - Charlemont (20-30)

Charlemont has gone to war against his father's wishes. When he is visited in a dream by his father's ghost, he awakens and questions the meaning of the strange experience.

CHARLEMONT: O my affrighted soul! what fearful dream
Was this that wak'd me? Dreams are but the rais'd
Impressions of premeditated things,
By serious apprehensions left upon
Our minds, or else th'imaginary shapes
Of objects proper to th'complexion, or
The dispositions of our bodies. These
Can neither of them be the cause, why I
Should dream thus; for my mind has not been mov'd
With any one conception of a thought
To such a purpose; nor my nature wont
To trouble me with fantasies of terror.
It must be something that my genius would
Inform me of. Now gracious Heaven forbid!
O! let my spirit be depriv'd of all
Foresight and knowledge, ere it understand
That vision acted; or divine that act
To come. Why should I think so? Left I not
My worthy father i'the kind regard
Of a most loving uncle? Soldier! sawst
No apparition of a man?
[SOLDIER: You dream Sir; I saw nothing.]
CHARLEMONT: Tush. These idle dreams
Are fabulous. Our boiling fantasies
Like troubled waters falsify the shapes
Of things retain'd in them; and make 'em seem
Confounded, when they are distinguish'd. So
My actions daily conversant with war

THE ATHEIST'S TRAGEDY

(The argument of blood and death) had left
(Perhaps) th'imaginary presence of
Some bloody accident upon my mind;
Which mix'd confusedly with other thoughts,
(Whereof th'rememberance of my father might
Be one) presented all together, seem
Incorporate; as if his body were
The owner of that blood, the subject of
That death, when he's at Paris, and that blood
Shed here. It may be thus. I would not leave
The war, for reputation's sake, upon
An idle apprehension, a vain dream.

THE ATHEIST'S TRAGEDY
by Cyril Tourneur
A 16th century French baronial estate - D'Amville (40-50)

A man haunted by his evil past is here tormented by phantoms.

D'AMVILLE: Why dost thou stare upon me? Thou art not
The skull of him I murder'd. What has thou
To do to vex my conscience? Sure thou wert
The head of a most dogged usurer,
Th'art so uncharitable. And that bawd,
The sky, there; she could shut the windows and
The doors of this great chamber of the world;
And draw the curtains of the clouds between
Those lights and me about this bed of earth,
When that same strumpet murder & my self
Committed sin together. Then she could
Leave us i' the dark, till the close deed was done:
But now, that I begin
To feel the loathsome horror of my sin;
And (like a lecher empty'd of his lust)
desire to bury my face under my eyebrows, and would steal from my
shame unseen; she meets me i' the face with all her light corrupted
eyes,
To challenge payment o' me.—O behold!
Yonder's the ghost of old Montferrers in
A long white sheet, climbing yond' lofty mountain
To complain to Heav'n of me.—Montferrers!
'Pox o' fearfulness. 'Tis nothing but
A fair white cloud. Why, was I born a coward?
He lies that says so. Yet the count'nance of
A bloodless worm might ha' the courage now
To turn my blood to water.
The trembling motion of an aspen leaf
Would make me like the shadow of that leaf,
Lie shaking under 't. I could now commit

THE ATHEIST'S TRAGEDY

A murder, were it but to drink the fresh
Warm blood of him I murder'd; to supply
The want and weakness o' mine own; 'tis grown
So cold and phlegmatic.

THE KING, THE GREATEST ALCALDE
by Lope Felix de Vega Carpio
translated by John Garrett Underhill
Leon, Spain - Sancho (20-30)

Here, Sancho speaks of his love for the beautiful Elvira.

SANCHO: You noble pastures of
   Galicia,
Under the shadow of these mountain
   sides,
Whose skirts the Sil amid his rushes
   green
Would kiss, sustenance to the marshalled
   host
Of flowers, varied in a thousand hues,
   you give.
You birds that sing of love, you beasts
   that roam
More tender love in birds or beasts or
   flowers?
But since it is impossible to see
Aught else of all the sun looks down upon
More beautiful than my Elvira is,
Nor aught else may be born, so, being
   born,
Of her great beauty by necessity
My love is sprung, which from her favor
   draws
Its brightest glory; no greater beauty is,
No greater beauty and no greater love.
Alas, sweet lady, may your beauty grow
That so in me may grow the love I
   bear!
But ah! Most beautiful of them that
   toil,

THE KING, THE GREATEST ALCALDE

Since beauty cannot find in thee increase,
Nor loving in my heart betimes, then
    know
I love you for the beauty that you show,
There is naught else to such endearment
    binds.
The pallid sands of this swift rivulet
You turned but yesterday to gleaming
    pearls,
Setting your feet therein, lilies of snow;
While I cried out, because I scarce could
    see,
Unto the sun, your face, wherewith you
    shed
Such radiance of light—who would not
    stay—
That he should look upon the water there,
So all your beauty might be visible.
Linen, Elvira, you were washing linen,
Which all your labor never could make
    white
For magic of the hands you laid thereon.
And I, behind these chestnuts, gazed on
    you
With trembling, till suddenly I saw that
    love
Had handed you the bandage from his
    eyes,
In his rich favor given you to lave.
But heaven forbids that love should go
    unblinded
I' the world!...Oh God! But when
    shall come that day
(On which I too must die), when at the

THE KING, THE GREATEST ALCALDE

last
I say to her: "Elvira, you are mine!"
What gifts and presents I shall shower on
    you!
I am no fool not to esteem your worth,
Each year more priceless dear in my
    affection.
Know in the realms of my heart's rich
    possession,
There are no provinces of mean disdain.

THE CID
by Pierre Corneille
translated by Florence Kendrick Cooper
Seville - Diègue (50-60)

The noble father of Roderick—the Cid—here defends his son to the king, who believes that Roderick has killed the Count of Gormaz. Diègue takes responsibility for the murder and asks that he be punished in his son's place.

DIÈGUE: Worthy of envy he
Who, losing life's best gift, can part with life!
For age's weakness brings to noble souls
A mournful fate before its closing scene.
I, whose proud 'scutcheon is graved o'er with deeds
I, whom a victor laurels oft have crowned,
To-day, because too long with life I've stayed
Affronted, prostrate lie and powerless.
What neither siege nor fight nor ambuscade,
Nor all your foes, nor all my envious friends,
Nor Aragon could do, nor proud Granada,
The count, your subject, jealous of your choice,
Bold in the power which youth has over age,
Has done within your court, beneath your eye.
Thus, sire, these locks, 'neath war's rough harness blanched,
This blood, so gladly lavished in your cause,
This arm, the lifelong terror of your foes,

THE CID

To a dishonored grave would have descended,
Had not my son proved worthy of his
    sire,
An honor to his country and his king.
He took his father's sword, he slew the
    count
He gave me back my honor cleansed from
    stain.
If to show courage and resentment deep,
If to avenge a blow, claim punishment,
On me alone should fall your anger's
    stroke.
When the arm errs, the head must bear
    the blame.
Whether this be a crime of which we
    speak,
His was the hand, but mine, sire, was the
    will.
Chimène names him her father's murderer;
The deed was mine; I longed to take his
    place.
Spare for your throne the arm of youth
    and might
But slay the chief whom Time o'ermasters
    soon.
If an old soldier's blood will expiate
And satisfy Chimène, 't is hers to shed;
Far from repining at such stern decree,
I'll glory in an honorable death.

THE CHANGELING
by Thomas Middleton and William Rowley
Allegant, a seaport on the east coast of Spain - Deflores (20-40)
   The ugly Delores here speaks of his love and lust for his
   mistress.

DEFLORES: *(Aside)* Younder's she.
Whatever ails me, now alate especially,
I can as well be hang'd as refrain seeing her;
Some twenty times a day, nay not so little,
Do I force errands, frame ways and excuses
To come into her sight, and I have
Small reason for't, and less encouragement;
For she baits me still
Every time worse than other, does profess herself
The cruellest enemy of my face in town,
At no hand can abide the sight of me,
As if danger, or ill luck hung in my looks.
I must confess my face is bad enough,
But I know far worse has better fortune,
And not endur'd alone, but dotes on,
And yet such pick-hair'd faces, chins like witches',
Here and there five hairs, whispering in a corner,
As if they grew in fear of one another,
Wrinkles like troughs, where swine deformity swills
The tears of perjury that lie there like wash,
Fallen from the slimy and dishonest eye,—
Yet such a one pluck'd sweets without restraint,
And has the grace of beauty to his sweet.
Though my hard fate has thrust me out to servitude,
I tumbled into th'world a gentleman.
She turns her blessed eye upon me now,
And I'll endure all storms before I part with't.
[BEATRICE: *(Aside)* Again—
This ominous ill-fac'd fellow more disturbs me,
Than all my other passions.]
DEFLORES: *(Aside)* Now't begins again,
I'll stand this storm of hail though the stones pelt me.

WOMEN BEWARE WOMEN
by Thomas Middleton
Florence - Leantino (3040)

When his wife leaves him to become the Duke's concubine,
Leantino grieves her loss.

LEANTINO: Is she my wife till death? yet no more mine?
That's a hard measure; then what's marriage good for?
Me thinks by right I should not now be living,
And then 'twere all well: what a happiness
Had I been made of, had I never seen her!
For nothing makes man's loss grievous to him,
But knowledge of the worth of what he loses;
For what he never had he never misses:
She's gone for ever, utterly; there is
As much redempdon of a soul from hell,
As a fair woman's body from his palace.
Why should my love last longer than her truth?
What is there good in woman to be lov'd,
When only that which makes her so has left her?
I cannot love her now, but I must like
Her sin, and my own shame too, and be guilty
Of law's breach with her, and mine own abusing;
All which were monstrous: then my safest course;
For health of mind and body, is to turn
My heart, and hate her, most extremely hate her;
I have no other way: those virtuous powers,
Which were chaste witnesses of both our troths,
Can witness she breaks first, and I'm rewarded
With captainship o'th'fort; a place of credit
I must confess, but poor; my factorship
Shall not exchange means with't: he that di'd last in't,
He was no drunkard, yet he di'd a beggar
For all his thrift; besides, the place not fits me;
It suits my resolution, not my breeding

JEPPE OF THE HILL
by Ludvig Holberg
translated by M. Jagendorf
Rural 18th century Denmark - Jeppe (30-50)

Following a rather blistering dressing-down from his nagging
wife, Jeppe bemoans his fate.

JEPPE: Look at that sow going in to eat her breakfast while I, poor
fool, must walk four miles without food or drink. I don't think there
is another man cursed with such a witch. I honestly think she is first
cousin to Satan. Everybody in the village says Jeppe drinks, but no
one says why Jeppe drinks. In the ten years I was in the militia I
didn't get the beatings I get in one day from my snake of a wife.
She beats me; the bailiff drives me to work as if I were a beast, and
the deacon makes a cuckold of me. Haven't I good reason to get
drunk? Mustn't I use every means in nature to forget my troubles?
If I were a fool I wouldn't take it so to heart; then I wouldn't have
to drink. But everyone knows I am a very bright fellow, and I feel
these things much more than others. That is why I must drink. My
neighbor Moens Christoffersen, he is my friend, he often says to me:
"Put the devil of courage in your big belly, Jeppe. You must learn
to hit good and hard, then your wife'll soon have to behave." But
I can't hit good and hard, and that for three reasons. First, I have
no courage, second, because of that accursed Master Eric who is
always hanging behind the bed. Just to think of him makes my back
weep bitter tears. And third, if I say it myself, because I have a
kind soul, and I am a good Christian. That's why I never try to take
revenge. Even on the deacon. I pay my offerings regularly on all
high holidays while he hasn't the decency to offer me a glass of beer
on any ordinary week day of the year. But nothing ever hurt me so
much as that insult last year when I told him a wild bull who wasn't
afraid of any man suddenly got scared of me. Said he to me: "Don't
you understand, Jeppe, why that happened? The bull saw that your
horns were even bigger than his and he thought it best not to butt
against one stronger than himself." I call

you to witness, good people, if such words wouldn't cut a decent man to the very bone and marrow. I am so honorable I don't even wish my wife to die. On the contrary. When she lay sick last year of the yellow jaundice, I wanted her to go on living. For since hell is already full of ugly women, Lucifer would send her back and then she'd be worse than before. But if the deacon dies, I'd be happy— for my sake as well as for others. He brings me only aggravation and is of no use to the parish. He is an ignorant devil. He can't sing a decent note, and can't pour a straight candle. Ah, but his predecessor! Christoffer! There was fellow of a different cut. He shouted his religion so you'd hear him over a dozen deacons put together. That's the kind of a voice he had. Yes, Moens Christoffersen, you and my other peasant neighbors, you can say lots of things but you have no Master Eric hanging behind your beds. If I had one wish in this whole world it'd be that my wife had no arm or I no back. Talk she can all she wants....But while I am on my way I might as well drop in on Jacob Skoemager. Perhaps he'll give me a shilling's worth of brandy on credit. After all I must take something to strengthen my body.

JEPPE OF THE HILL
by Ludvig Holberg
translated by M. Jagendorf
Rural 18th century Denmark - Jeppe (30-50)

When the Baron and his men discover Jeppe fast asleep in the middle of the road, they decide to put him in the Baron's clothes and bed for jest. Here, the confused Jeppe awakens in the Baron's sumptuous bedchamber and questions his sanity.

JEPPE: What's all this? What glory! How did I get here? Am I dreaming or am I awake? No,—wide-awake. Where are my wife and children? Where is my home, and where is Jeppe? Everything has changed; I too. What does it all mean? *(Calling in a faint and frightened voice.)* Nille! Nille! Nille! I believe I've come to heaven, Nille, by some accident. But is this really me? I think it is, and then again I think it isn't. If I feel my back that's still aching from the beatings I got, if I hear myself speaking, if I stick my tongue in the holes in my teeth, then I believe it's me; but if I look at my cap, at my shirt and all the other beautiful things I see, when I hear that sweet music, devil take it if I can get it through my noodle that it is me. No, it's not me. I'll be cursed a thousand times if it's me. But perhaps I'm dreaming? No, I don't believe it. I'll pinch myself in the arm. If it doesn't hurt then I'm dreaming. If it does, then I'm not dreaming. *(Pinches himself.)* Yes, I felt it, so I'm awake. I'm honestly awake. None can argue me out of that. For if I wasn't I couldn't....But when I think of it, how can I be awake? It's positive that I am Jeppe of the Hill. I know I am a poor peasant, a dolt, a knave, a cuckold, a hungry louse, a bit of vermin and a scoundrel—then how can I be emperor and lord of a castle? No, it's only a dream. The best thing is to be patient until I wake up. *(The music commences again to play and JEPPE weeps again.)* Can anything like that be heard in a dream? But it's impossible. If it's only a dream I wish I'd never wake again; and if I've gone crazy I don't want to ever be sane again. I'd drag any doctor who'd want to cure me before a judge. I'd curse anyone who'd wake me. But I'm neither dreaming nor crazy. I can remember that my father, God bless his soul, was Niels of the Hill; my grandfather, Jeppe of the Hill. My wife's name is Nille, and she has a whip called Master Eric. My sons' names are Hans, Christoffer and Niels. But wait a minute, I've got it. It's the eternal life. It's paradise. This is the heavenly kingdom. Probably I drank too much once again at Jacob Skoemager's, died and went straight to heaven. Dying isn't so hard as people make it out. I for one didn't feel a single thing. Perhaps at this very minute the pastor is standing in the pulpit and delivering a funeral sermon over me, saying: "That is the end of Jeppe of the Hill. He lived like a soldier and died like a soldier." They could argue whether I died on land or sea. I know I was quite wet when I left the world. Aha, Jeppe, that's very different from running four miles to town to buy soap. It's different from sleeping on straw, getting beatings from your wife and horns from the deacon. Oh, into what a happy life your hardships and misery have turned! I could cry from sheer joy, particularly when I think how I didn't deserve it. But one thing bothers me: I'm so thirsty my lips are glued together. If I desired to live again it'd be only to get a pitcher of beer. For what's the good of all the finery before my eyes and ears if I'm going to suffer of thirst. I remember the pastor used to say: "In heaven there is neither hunger nor thirst, and you'll meet there all your dead friends." But I am dying of thirst and I'm all alone—I don't see a soul. I thought I'd find at least my grandfather here; he was so fine a man that he died, and didn't owe a shilling to his lordship. I also know that other people lived as honest as I. Then why am I the only one in heaven? It can't be heaven. Then what is it? I'm not asleep; I'm not awake; I'm not dead; I'm not alive; I'm not crazy, I am not sane; I'm Jeppe of the Hill; I'm not Jeppe of the Hill. I am poor; I am rich; I am a miserable peasant; I am an emperor. *(Roaring.)* O...o...ah....Help! Help! Help!

MISS SARA SAMPSON
by Gotthold Ephraim Lessing
translated by Ernest Bell
A room in an inn - Mellefont (30's)

A notorious womanizer, Mellefont has finally fallen in love with
the virtuous young Sara. Even so, he cannot seem to make a
commitment to her.

MELLEFONT: *(after walking up and down several times in
thought.)* What a riddle I am to myself! What shall I think myself?
A fool? Or a knave? Heart, what a villain thou art! I love the
angel, however much of a devil I may be. I love her! Yes,
certainly! certainly I love her. I feel I would sacrifice a thousand
lives for her, for her who sacrificed her virtue for me; I would do
so,—this very moment without hesitation would I do so. And yet,
yet—I am afraid to say it to myself—and yet—how shall I explain it?
And yet I fear the moment which will make her mine for ever before
the world. It cannot be avoided now, for her father is reconciled.
Nor shall I be able to put it off for long. The delay has already
drawn down painful reproaches enough upon me. But painful as
they were, they were still more supportable to me than the melancholy thought of being fettered for life. But am I not so already?
Certainly,—and with pleasure! Certainly I am already her prisoner.
What is it I want, then? At present I am a prisoner, who is allowed
to go about on parole; that is flattering! Why cannot the matter rest
there? Why must I be put in chains and thus lack even the pitiable
shadow of freedom? In chains? Quite so! Sara Sampson, my
beloved! What bliss lies in these words! Sara Sampson, my wife!
The half of the bliss is gone! and the other half—will go! Monster
that I am! And with such thoughts shall I write to her father? Yet
these are not my real thoughts, they are fancies! Cursed fancies,
which have become natural to me through my dissolute life! I will
free myself from them, or live no more.

SAUL
by Vittorio Alfieri
translated by E.A. Bowring
Israelies' camp in Gilboa - David (30-40)

On the eve of the battle between the Israelites and the
Philistines, David—a onetime favorite of Saul—addresses his
concerns for the future to God.

DAVID: Here, God Omnipotent, wilt
    Thou that I
Restrain that course to which Thou hast
    impell'd me ?
Here will I stand.—These are Gilboa's
    mountains,
Now forming Israel's camp, exposed in
    front
To the profane Philistines. Ah, that I
Might fall to-day beneath the foeman's
    sword!
But, death awaits me from the hand of
    Saul.
Ah, cruel and infatuated Saul!
Who, without giving him a moment's
    respite,
Through caverns, and o'er cliffs, dost chase
    thy champion.
And yet the self-same David formerly
Was thy defender; all thy confidence
In me hadst thou reposed; me didst thou
    raise
To honor's pinnacle; and as a spouse
I was by thee selected for thy daughter...
But, as an inauspicious dowry, thou
Didst ask of me, dissever'd from thy foes,
A hundred heads: and I have brought of
    them

SAUL

To thee, full faithfully, a double harvest...
But Saul, I clearly see, in thought is
    stricken;
Long hath he been so: to an evil spirit
His God abandons his perverted mind:
O Heav'ns! Distracted mortals! what are
    we,
If God forsakes us?—Night, do thou soon
    yield
Thy shades to the glad sun; for he to-day
The witness of a gen'rous enterprise
Is destined to shine forth. Gilboa, thou
Shalt, to the latest ages, be renown'd;
They shall record of thee, that David here
Himself surrender'd to ferocious Saul.—
March forth, O Israel, from thy peaceful
    tents;
March forth from them, O king: I challenge
    you
To-day to witness, if I yet am versed
In military arts. And march thou forth,
Impious Philistia; march thou forth, and
    see
Whether my sword have yet the pow'r to
    smite.

EGMONT
by Johann Wolfgang Goethe
translated by Anna Swanwick
Brussels - Brackenburg (20's)

While his people threaten to revolt against Spanish rule, passionate young Brackenburg laments an unrequited love.

BRACKENBURG: *(alone.)* I had resolved to go away again at once, and yet, when she takes me at my word, and lets me leave her, I feel as if I could go mad.— Wretched man! Does the fate of thy fatherland, does the growing disturbance fail to move thee?—Are countryman and Spaniard the same to thee? and carest thou not who rules, and who is in the right?—I was a different sort of fellow as a schoolboy!—Then, when an exercise in oratory was given; "Brutus' speech for liberty," for instance, Fritz was ever the first, and the rector would say: "If it were only spoken more deliberately, the words not all huddled together."—Then my blood boiled, and I longed for action;—Now I drag along, bound by the eyes of a maiden. I cannot leave her! yet she, alas, cannot love me!—ah— no—she—she cannot have entirely rejected me—not entirely—yet half love is no love!—I will endure it no longer!—Can it be true what a friend lately whispered in my ear that she secretly admits a man into the house by night, when she always sends me away modestly before evening? No, it cannot be true! It is a lie! A base, slanderous, lie! Clara is as innocent as I am wretched.—She has rejected me, has thrust me from her heart—and shall I live on thus? I cannot, I will not endure it. Already my native land is convulsed by internal strife, and do I perish abjectly amid the tumult? I will not endure it! When the trumpet sounds, when a shot falls, it thrills through my bone and marrow! But, alas, it does not rouse me! It does not summon me to join the onslaught, to rescue, to dare.—Wretched, degrading position! Better end it at once! Not long ago, I threw myself into the water; I sank—but nature in her agony was too strong for me; I felt that I could swim, and saved myself against my will. Could I but forget the time when she loved me, seemed to love

67

me!—Why has this happiness penetrated my very bone and marrow? Why have these hopes, while disclosing to me a distant paradise, consumed all the enjoyment of life?—and that first, that only kiss!— Here *(Laying his hand upon the table.),* here we were alone,—she had always been kind and friendly towards me,—then she seemed to soften,—she looked at me,—my brain reeled,—I felt her lips on mine,—and—and now?—Die, wretch! Why dost thou hesitate? *(He draws a phial from his pocket.)* Thou healing poison, it shall not have been in vain that I stole thee from my brother's medicine chest! From this anxious fear, this dizziness, this death-agony, thou shalt deliver me at once.

EGMONT
by Johann Wolfgang Goethe
translated by Anna Swanwick
Brussels - Egmont (30's)

Count Egmont has led the rebellion against Spanish rule in the Netherlands. Captured and sentenced to death, Egmont bravely faces his executioners.

EGMONT: The crown is vanished! Beautiful vision, the light of day has frighted thee! Yes, they revealed themselves to my sight, uniting in one radiant form the two sweetest joys of my heart. Divine Liberty borrowed the mien of my beloved one; the lovely maiden arrayed herself in the celestial garb of her friend. In a solemn moment they appeared united with aspect more earnest than tender. With bloodstained feet the vision approached, the waving folds of her robe also were tinted with blood. It was my blood, and the blood of many brave hearts. No! It shall not be shed in vain! Forward! Brave people! The goddess of liberty leads you on! And as the sea breaks through and destroys the barriers that would oppose its fury, so do ye overwhelm the bulwark of tyranny, and with your impetuous flood sweep it away from the land which it usurps.

(Drums.)

Hark! Hark! How often has this sound summoned my joyous steps to the field of battle and of victory! How bravely did I tread, with my gallant comrades, the dangerous path of fame! And now, from this dungeon I shall go forth, to meet a glorious death; I die for freedom, for whose cause I have lived and fought, and for whom I now offer myself up a sorrowing sacrifice.

(The back-ground is occupied by Spanish soldiers with halberts.)

Yes, lead them on! Close your ranks, ye terrify me not. I am accustomed to stand amid the serried ranks of war, and environed by the threatening forms of death, to feel, with double zest, the energy of life.

(Drums.)

The foe closes round on every side! Swords are flashing; courage, friends! Behind are your parents, your wives, your children!

69

(Pointing to the guard.)

And these are impelled by the word of their leader, not by their own free will. Protect your homes! And to save those who are most dear to you, be ready to follow my example, and to fall with joy. *(Drums. As he advances through the guards towards the door in the back-ground, the curtain falls. The music joins in, and the scene closes with a symphony of victory.)*

WILLIAM TELL
by Johann Christoph Friedrich von Schiller
translated by Sir Theodore Martin
A woods in 14th century Switzerland - William Tell

A Swiss patriot leading the rebellion against Austrian rule, Tell
here lies in wait for his enemy, Gessler.

TELL: *(enters with his cross-bow.)* Here
    thro' this deep defile he needs must
    pass;
There leads no other road to Kussnacht:
    —here
I'll do it:—the opportunity is good.
Yon alder tree stands well for my concealment.
Thence my avenging shaft will surely
    reach him;
The straitness of the path forbids pursuit.
Now, Gessler, balance thine account with
    Heaven!
Thou must away from earth,—thy sand is
    run.
I led a peaceful, inoffensive life;—
My bow was bent on forest game alone,
And my pure soul was free from thoughts
    of murder—
But thou hast scared me from my dream
    of peace;
The milk of human kindness thou hast
    turn'd
To rankling poison in my breast, and
    made
Appalling deeds familiar to my soul.
He who could make his own child's head
    his mark
Can speed his arrow to his foeman's heart.

WILLIAM TELL

My children dear, my lov'd and faithful
    wife
Must be protected, tyrant, from thy
    fury!—
When last I drew my bow—with trembling
    hand—
And thou, with murderous joy, a father
    forced
To level at his child—when, all in vain,
Writhing before thee, I implored thy
    mercy—
Then in the agony of my soul I vow'd
A fearful oath, which met God's ear
    alone,
That when my bow next wing'd an arrow's
    flight
Its aim should be thy heart. The vow I
    made,
Amid the hellish torments of that moment,
I hold a sacred debt, and I will pay it.
Thou art my lord, my Emperor's delegate;
Yet would the Emperor not have stretch'd
    his power
So far as thou. He sent thee to these
    Cantons
To deal forth law—stern law—for he is
    anger'd;
But not to wanton with unbridled will
In every cruelty, with fiend-like joy:—
There is a God to punish and avenge.
Come forth, thou bringer once of bitter
    pangs;
precious jewel now,—my chiefest
    treasure—

WILLIAM TELL

A mark I'll set thee, which the cry of
    grief
Could never penetrate,—but thou shalt
    pierce it.—
And thou, my trusty bowstring, that so
    oft
Has served me faithfully in sportive
    scenes,
Desert me not in this most serious hour—
Only be true this once, my own good cord,
That hast so often wing'd the biting
    shaft:—
For shouldst thou fly successless from my
    hand,
I have no second to send after thee.

(Travellers pass over the stage.)

I'll sit me down upon this bench of
    stone,
Hewn for the wayworn traveller's brief
    repose—
For here there is no home.—Each hurries
    by
The other, with quick step and careless
    look,
Nor stays to question of his grief.—Here
    goes
The merchant, full of care,—the pilgrim,
    next,
With slender scrip,—and then the pious
    monk.
The scowling robber, the jovial player,
The carrier with his heavy-laden horse,
That comes to us from the far haunts of
    men;

WILLIAM TELL

For every road conducts to the world's
    end.
They all push onwards—every man intent
On his own several business—mine is
    murder.   *(Sits down.)*
Time was, my dearest children, when
    with joy
You hail'd your father's safe return to
    home
From his long mountain toils; for, when
    he came,
He ever brought some little present with
    him.
A lovely Alpine flower—a curious bird—
Or elf-boat, found by wanderer on the
    hills.—
But now he goes in quest of other game:
In the wild pass he sits, and broods on
    murder,
And watches for the life-blood of his
    foe.—
But still his thoughts are fixed on you
    alone,
Dear children.—'Tis to guard your innocence,
To shield you from the tyrant's fell revenge,
He bends his bow to do a deed of blood!

                              (Rises.)

Well—I am watching for a noble prey—
Does not the huntsman, with severest toil,
Roam for whole days, amid the winter's
    cold,
Leap with a daring bound from rock to
    rock,
And climb the jagged, slippery steeps, to
    which

74

WILLIAM TELL

His limbs are glued by his own streaming
    blood—
And all this but to gain a wretched
    chamois.
A far more precious prize is now my
    aim—
The heart of that dire foe who would
    destroy me.

*(Sprightly music heard in the
distance, which comes gradually
nearer.)*

From my first years of boyhood I have
    used
The bow—been practised in the archer's
    feats;
The bull's eye many a time my shafts
    have hit,
And many a goodly prize have I brought
    home,
Won in the games of skill.—This day I'll
    make
My master-shot, and win the highest prize
Within the whole circumference of the
    mountains.

HERNANI
by Victor Hugo
translated by Mrs. Newton Crosland

Castle of Silva in the mountains of Aragon - Don Ruy Gomez (50-60)

The don desires to marry his beautiful young niece. Here, he tells her of his desire to be young again.

DON RUY GOMEZ: *(rising, and going*
    toward her.) Now list. One cannot be
The master of himself, so much in love
As I am now with thee. And I am old
And jealous, and am cross—and why?
    Because
I'm old; because the beauty, grace, or
    youth
Of others frightens, threatens me. Because,
While jealous thus of others, of myself
I am ashamed. What mockery! that this
    love
Which to the heart brings back such joy
    and warmth
Should halt, and but rejuvenate the soul,
Forgetful of the body. When I see
A youthful peasant, singing blithe and
    gay,
In the green meadows, often then I muse—
I, in my dismal paths, and murmur low:
Oh, I would give my battlemented towers,
And ancient ducal donjon, and my fields
Of corn, and all my forest lands, and
    flocks
So vast which feed upon my hills, my
    name
And all my ancient titles—ruins mine,

HERNANI

And ancestors who must expect me soon,
All—all I'd give for his new cot, and brow
Unwrinkled. For his hair is raven black,
And his eyes shine like yours. Beholding
　　him
You might exclaim: A young man this!
　　And then
Would think of me so old. I know it
　　well.
I am named Silva. Ah, but that is not
Enough; I say it, see it. Now behold
To what excess I love thee. All I'd give
Could I be like thee—young and handsome
　　now!
Vain dream! that I were young again,
　　who must
By long, long years precede thee to the
　　tomb.
[DOÑA SOL: Who knows?]
DON RUY GOMEZ: And yet, I pray you,
　　me believe,
The frivolous swains have not so much of
　　love
Within their hearts as on their tongues.
　　A girl
May love and trust one; if she dies for
　　him,
He laughs. The strong-winged and gay-
　　painted birds
That warble sweet, and in the thicket
　　trill,
Will change their loves as they their
　　plumage moult.
They are the old, with voice and color
　　gone,

And beauty fled, who have the resting
    wings
We love the best. Our steps are slow,
    and dim
Our eyes. Our brows are furrowed,—but
    the heart
Is never wrinkled. When an old man
    loves
He should be spared. The heart is ever
    young,
And always it can bleed. This love of
    mine
Is not a plaything made of glass to shake
And break. It is a love severe and sure,
Solid, profound, paternal,—strong as is
The oak which forms my ducal chair. See,
    then,
How well I love thee—and in other ways
I love thee—hundred other ways, e'en as
We love the dawn, and flowers, and
    heaven's blue!
To see thee, mark thy graceful step each
    day,
Thy forehead pure, thy brightly beaming
    eye,
I'm joyous—feeling that my soul will
    have
Perpetual festival!

UNCLE TOM'S CABIN
by George L. Aiken
Louisiana - Simon Legree (40-50)

The notoriously cruel Legree here reveals the source of his evil nature to Cassie, his slave and concubine.

LEGREE: Cassy, tonight the past has been recalled to me—the past that I have so long and vainly striven to forget.

[CASSY: Has aught on this earth power to move a soul like thine?]

LEGREE: [Yes,] for hard and reprobate as I now seem, there has been a time when I have been rocked on the bosom of mother, cradled with prayers and pious hymns, my now seared brow bedewed with the waters of holy baptism.

[CASSY: *(Aside.)* What sweet memories of childhood can thus soften down that heart of iron?]

LEGREE: In early childhood a fair-haired woman has led me, at the sound of Sabbath bells, to worship and to pray. Born of a hard-tempered sire, on whom that gentle woman had wasted a world of unvalued love, I followed in the steps of my father. Boisterous, unruly and tyrannical I despised all her counsel, and would have none of her reproof, and at an early age, broke from her to seek my fortunes on the sea. I never came home but once after that; and then my mother, with the yearning of a heart that must love something, and had nothing else to love clung to me, and sought with passionate prayers and entreaties to win me from a life of sin.

[CASSY: That was your day of grace, Legree; then good angels called you and mercy held you by the hand.]

LEGREE: My heart inly relented; there was a conflict, but sin got the victory, and I set all the force of my rough nature against the conviction of my conscience. I drank and swore, was wilder and more brutal than ever. And one night, when my mother, in the last agony of her despair, knelt at my feet, I spurned her from me, threw her senseless on the floor, and with brutal curses fled to my ship.

[CASSY: Then the fiend took thee for his own.]

LEGREE: The next I heard of my mother was one night while I

was carousing among drunken companions. A letter was put in my hands. I opened it, and a lock of long, curling hair fell from it, and twined about my fingers even as that lock twined but now. The letter told me that my mother was dead, and that dying she blest and forgave me! *(Buries his face in his hands.)*

[CASSY: Why did you not even then renounce your evil ways?]

LEGREE: There is a dread, unhallowed necromancy of evil, that turns things sweetest and holiest to phantoms of horror and afright. That pale, loving mother,—her dying prayers, her forgiving love,— wrought in my demoniac heart of sin only as a damning sentence, bringing with it a fearful looking for of judgement and fiery indignation.

[CASSY: And yet you would not strive to avert the doom that threatened you.]

LEGREE: I burned the lock of hair and I burned the letter; and when I saw them hissing and crackling in the flame, inly shuddered as I thought of everlasting fires! I tried to drink and revel, and wear away the memory; but often in the deep night, whose solemn stillness arraigns the soul in forced communion with itself, I have seen that pale mother rising by my bed-side, and felt the soft twining of that hair around my fingers, 'till the cold sweat would roll down my face, and I would spring from my bed in horror—horror! *(Falls in chair—After a pause.)* What the devil ails me? Large drops of sweat stand on my forehead, and my heart beats heavy and thick with fear. I thought I saw something white rising and glimmering in the gloom before me, and it seemed to bear my mother's face! I know one thing; I'll let that fellow Tom alone after this. What did I want with his cussed paper? I believe I am bewitched sure enough! I've been shivering and sweating ever since! Where did he get that hair? It couldn't have been that! I *burn'd* that up, I know I did! It would be a joke if hair could rise from the dead! I'll have Sambo and Quimbo up here to sing and dance one of their dances and keep off these horrid notions.

THE DEMI-MONDE
by Alexandre Dumas Fils
translated by Harold Harper
19th Century Paris - Oliver (30-40)

The rakish Oliver here offers an insightful interpretation of Parisian society.

OLIVER: My dear fellow, you must live for a long time, as I have, in the intimate circles of Parisian society in order to understand the various shades of this particular stratum. It is not easy to explain.— Do you like peaches?

[RAYMOND: *(surprised.)* Peaches? Yes.]

OLIVIER: Well, go to a large fruit dealer, Chevet's, say, or Potel's, and ask for his best peaches. He will show you a basket of magnificent ones, each one separated from the other by leaves, in order to keep them from touching, from decaying by the contact. Ask him the price, and he will tell you: "Thirty sous each," I imagine. Look about you then and you will not fail to see another basket filled with peaches looking at first sight exactly like the others, but they are packed closer together; only one side is visible. The dealer will not offer you these. Ask him their price, and he will reply: "Fifteen sous." You will naturally ask why these peaches, as large, as beautiful and ripe as the others, are cheaper. Then he will pick one up with the tips of his fingers as delicately as he can, turn it around, and show you on the bottom a tiny black speck. That is the explanation of the lower price. My dear fellow, you are now in the fifteen-sous peach basket. Each woman here has some blot in her past life; they are crowded close to one another in order that these blots may be noticed as little as possible. Although they have the same origin, the same appearance and the same prejudices as women of society, they do not belong to it: they constitute the "Demi-monde" or "Half-world," a veritable floating island on the ocean of Paris, which calls to itself, welcomes, accepts everything that falls, emigrates, everything that escapes from *terra firma* - not to mention those who have been shipwrecked or who come from God knows where.

[RAYMOND: And has this social stratum any particular visible characteristics?]

OLIVER: You see it everywhere, but rather indistinctly; a Parisian can recognize it at a glance.

[RAYMOND: How?]

OLIVER: By the absence of husbands. It is full of married women whose husbands are never seen.

[RAYMOND: But what is the origin of this strange social world?]

OLIVER: It is a modern creation. In former times adultery as we now think of it, did not exist: morals were much more lax; there was a word much more trivial to denote what is now thought of as adultery. Molière made frequent use of it, and made rather the husband ridiculous than the wife at fault. But since the husband, aided by the law, has acquired the right to expel the erring wife from his home, a modification of the manner of looking at such things has come, and this modification has created a new society. What was to become of all these compromised and repudiated wives? The first who saw herself sent from the conjugal roof went into distant retirement somewhere to hide her grief and shame; but—the second? The second followed the first, and the two gave the name of misfortune to what was really a fault; an error to what was actually a crime. They began to console and excuse each other. With the advent of a third, they invited one another to lunch; with the fourth, they had a dance. Then about this nucleus came in turn young girls who have "made a false step," questionable widows, women who bear the name of the man they are living with, some truly-married couples who made their *début* in a *liaison* of many years' standing; finally, the women who think they have done something of importance and who do not want to appear as they really are. To-day this irregular society functions regularly; this bastard society holds charms for the younger generation. "Love" is more easily obtained than higher up, and cheaper than at the bottom.

[RAYMOND: Where do these people go?]

THE DEMI-MONDE

OLIVER: It's impossible to say. Only, beneath the brilliant surface, gilded by youth, beauty, money, under this social fabric of laces, smiles, fetes, and passion, dark and tragic dramas are played, dramas of expiation, scandal, ruin, of the dishonor of whole families, law-suits, children separated from their mothers, children who are forced to forget them at an early age in order not to curse them later on. Then youth passes away, lovers disappear, and out of the past come regrets, remorse, abandonment, and solitude. Among these women are some who attach themselves to men who have been fools enough to take them seriously; they ruin the lives of these men as they have ruined their own; others disappear and no one ever troubles to find out where they have gone. Some cling to this society—like the Viscountess de Vernieres—and die not knowing whether they prefer to rise or fear to fall; others, either because they sincerely repent or because they fear the desert about them, pray, in the name of their children or on behalf of the good of the family, to be taken back by their husbands. Then friends intervene and a few good reasons are set forth: the wife is old, people will not gossip about her. The ruined marriage is patched up again, the facade is given a new coat of paint, the couple go to the country for a year or two; they return, society closes its eyes, and allows from time to time those who publicly went out by the front door to creep in through the small door at the back.

MISS JULIE
by August Strindberg
translated by Evert Sprinchorn
Count's manor house - 19th century Sweden - Jean (20-30)

Jean, a servant, has been in love with the Count's daughter since
they both were children. Here, he confesses his feelings to her.

JEAN: We don't use that word around here. But I've
been—interested in a lot of girls, if that's what you mean....I even
got sick once because I couldn't have the one I wanted—really sick,
like the princes in the Arabian Nights—who couldn't eat or drink for
love.

[MISS JULIE: Who was the girl? *(JEAN does not reply)* Who was
she?]

JEAN: You can't make me tell you that.

[MISS JULIE: Even if I ask you as an equal—ask you—as a friend?
...Who was she?]

JEAN: You.

[MISS JULIE: *(sitting down)* How—amusing...]

JEAN: Yes, maybe so. Ridiculous...That's why I didn't want to
tell you about it before. But now I'll tell you the whole story...Have
you any idea what the world looks like from below? Of course you
haven't. No more than a hawk or eagle has. You hardly ever see
their backs because they're always soaring above us. I lived with
seven brothers and sisters—and a pig—out on the waste land where
there wasn't even a tree growing. But from my window I could see
the wall of the Count's garden with the apple trees sticking up over
it. That was the Garden of Eden for me, and there were many angry
angels with flaming swords standing guard over it. But in spite of
them, I and the other boys found a way to the Tree of Life...I'll bet
you despise me.

[MISS JULIE: All boys steal apples.]

JEAN: That's what you say now. But you still despise me. Never
mind. One day I went with my mother into this paradise to weed
the onion beds. Next to the vegetable garden stood a Turkish

84

pavilion, shaded by jasmine and hung all over with honeysuckle. I couldn't imagine what it was used for. I only knew I had never seen such a beautiful building. People went in, and came out again. And one day the door was left open. I sneaked in. The walls were covered with portraits of kings and emperors, and the windows had red curtains with tassels on them.—You do know what kind of place I'm talking about, don't you...I—*(He breaks off a lilac and holds it under Miss Julie's nose)* I had never been inside a castle, never seen anything besides the church. But this was more beautiful. And no matter what I tried to think about, my thoughts always came back— to that little pavilion. And little by little there arose in me a desire to experience just for once the whole pleasure of...*Enfin*, I sneaked in, looked about, and marveled. Then I heard someone coming! There was only one way out—for the upper-class people. But for me there was one more—a lower one. And I had no other choice but to take it. *(MISS JULIE, who has taken the lilac from JEAN, lets it fall to the table)* Then I began to run like mad, plunging through the raspberry bushes, ploughing through the strawberry patches, and came up on the rose terrace. And there I caught sight of a pink dress and a pair of white stockings. That was you. I crawled under a pile of weeds, under—well, you can imagine what it was like—under thistles that pricked me and wet dirt that stank to high heaven. And all the while I could see you walking among the roses. I said to myself, "If it's true that a thief can enter heaven and be with the angels, isn't it strange that a poor man's child here on God's green earth can't enter the Count's park and play with the Count's daughter."

[MISS JULIE: *(sentimentally)* Do you think all poor children have felt that way?]

JEAN: *(hesitatingly at first, then with mounting conviction)* If all poor ch—? Yes—yes, naturally. Of course!

[MISS JULIE: It must be terrible to be poor.]

JEAN: *(with exaggerated pain and poignancy)* Oh, Miss Julie! You don't know! A dog can lie on the sofa with its mistress; a horse can have its nose stroked by the hand of a countess; but a servant—! *(changing his tone)* Of course, now and then you meet somebody with guts enough to work his way up in the world, but how often?—Anyway, you know what I did afterwards? I threw myself into the millstream with all my clothes on. Got fished out and spanked. But the following Sunday, when Pa and everybody else in the house went to visit Grandma, I arranged things so I'd be left behind. Then I washed myself all over with soap and warm water, put on my best clothes, and went off to church—just to see you there once more. I saw you, and then I went home determined to die. But I wanted to die beautifully and comfortably, without pain. I remembered that it was fatal to sleep under an alder bush. And we had a big one that had just blossomed out. I stripped it of every leaf and blossom it had and made a bed of them in a bin of oats. Have you ever noticed how smooth oats are? As smooth as the touch of human skin...So I pulled the lid of the bin shut and closed my eyes—fell asleep. And when they woke me I was really very sick. But I didn't die, as you can see.—What was I trying to prove? I don't know. There was no hope of winning you. But you were a symbol of the absolute hopelessness of my ever getting out of the circle I was born in.

SALOMÉ
by Oscar Wilde
The court of Herod - Herod (50-60)

Herod has promised Salomé whatever she desires in return for
dancing at his birthday feast. When she demands the head of
John the Baptist, Herod tries in vain to discourage her bloody
request.

HEROD: Thou art not listening. Thou art not listening. Suffer me
to speak, Salomé.
[SALOMÉ: The head of Jokanaan.]
HEROD: No, no, thou wouldst not have that. Thou sayest that but
to trouble me, because I have looked at thee and ceased not this
night. It is true, I have looked at thee and ceased not this night.
Thy beauty has troubled me. Thy beauty has grievously troubled
me, and I have looked at thee over-much. Nay, but I will look at
thee no more. One should not look at anything. Neither at things,
nor at people should one look. Only in mirrors is it well to look,
for mirrors do but show us masks. Oh! oh! bring wine! I thirst....
Salomé, Salomé, let us be as friends. Bethink thee....Ah! what
would I say? What was't? Ah! I remember it!...Salomé—nay but
come nearer to me; I fear thou wilt not hear my words—Salomé,
thou knowest my white peacocks, my beautiful white peacocks, that
walk in the garden between the myrtles and the tall cypress trees.
Their beaks are gilded with gold and the grains that they eat are
smeared with gold, and their feet are stained with purple. When
they cry out the rain comes, and the moon shows herself in the
heavens when they spread their tails. Two by two they walk
between the cypress trees and the black myrtles, and each has a slave
to tend it. Sometimes they fly across the trees, and anon they
crouch in the grass, and round the pools of the water. There are not
in all the world birds so wonderful. I know that Cæsar himself has
no birds so fair as my birds. I will give thee fifty of my peacocks.
They will follow thee whithersoever thou goest, and in the midst of
them thou wilt be like unto the moon in the midst of a great white

SALOMÉ

cloud....I will give them to thee all. I have but a hundred, and in the whole world there is no king who has peacocks like unto my peacocks. But I will give them all to thee. Only thou must loose me from my oath, and must not ask of me that which thy lips have asked of me. *(He empties the cup of wine.)*

[SALOMÉ: Give me the head of Jokanaan.]

[HERODIAS: Well said, my daughter! As for you, you are ridiculous with your peacocks.]

HEROD: Ah! thou are not listening to me. Be calm. As for me, am I not calm? I am altogether calm. Listen. I have jewels hidden in this palace—jewels that thy mother even has never seen; jewels that are marvellous to look at. I have a collar of pearls, set in four rows. They are like unto moons chained with rays of silver. They are even as half a hundred moons caught in a golden net. On the ivory breast of a queen they have rested. Thou shalt be as fair as a queen when thou wearest them. I have amethysts of two kinds, one that is black like wine, and one that is red like wine that one has coloured with water. I have topazes, yellow as are the eyes of tigers, and topazes that are pink as the eyes of a wood-pigeon, and green topazes that are as the eyes of cats. I have opals that burn always, with a flame that is cold as ice, opals that make sad men's minds, and are afraid of the shadows. I have onyxes like the eyeballs of a dead woman. I have moonstones that change when the moon changes, and are wan when they see the sun. I have sapphires big like eggs, and as blue as blue flowers. The sea wanders within them and the moon comes never to trouble the blue of their waves. I have chrysolites and beryls and chrysoprases and rubies. I have sardonyx and hyacinth stones, and stones of chalcedony, and I will give them all unto thee, all, and other things will I add to them. The King of the Indies has but even now sent me four fans fashioned from the feathers of parrots, and the King of Numidia a garment of ostrich feathers. I have a crystal, into which it is not lawful for a woman to look, nor may young men behold it until they have been beaten with rods. In a coffer of nacre I have three wondrous turquoises. He who wears them on his forehead can imagine things which are not, and he who carries them in his hand can turn the fruitful woman into a woman that is barren. These are great treasures above all price. But this is not all. In an ebony coffer I have two cups, amber, that are like apples of pure gold. If an enemy pour poison into these cups they become like apples of silver. In a coffer incrusted with amber I have sandals incrusted with glass. I have mantles that have been brought from the land of the Seres, and bracelets decked about with carbuncles and with jade that comes from the city of Euphrates....What desirest thou more than this, Salomé! Tell me the thing that thou desirest, and I will give it thee. All that thou askest I will give thee, save one thing only. I will give thee all that is mine, save only the head of one man. I will give thee the mantle of the high priest. I will give thee the veil of the sanctuary.

THE IMPORTANCE OF BEING EARNEST
A Trivial Comedy for Serious People
by Oscar Wilde
Late 19th century England - Jack (20-30)

The "gorgonesque" Lady Bracknell has declared that Jack may not court her niece. By way of retaliation, Jack here declares to his nemesis that he doesn't consider her beloved nephew a suitable suitor for *his* niece.

JACK: I beg your pardon for interrupting you, Lady Bracknell, but this engagement is quite out of the question. I am Miss Cardew's guardian, and she cannot marry without my consent until she comes of age. That consent I absolutely decline to give.

[LADY BRACKNELL: Upon what grounds, may I ask? Algernon is an extremely, I may almost say an ostentatiously, eligible young man. He has nothing, but he looks everything. What more can one desire?]

JACK: It pains me very much to have to speak frankly to you, Lady Bracknell, about your nephew, but the fact is that I do not approve at all of his moral character. I suspect him of being untruthful.

(ALGERNON and CECILY look at him in indignant amazement.)

[LADY BRACKNELL: Untruthful! My nephew Algernon? Impossible! He is an Oxonian.]

JACK: I fear there can be no possible doubt about the matter. This afternoon, during my temporary absence in London on an important question of romance, he obtained admission to my house by means of the false pretence of being my brother. Under an assumed name he drank, I've just been informed by my butler, an entire pint bottle of my Perrier-Jouet, Brut, '89; a wine I was specially reserving for myself. Continuing his disgraceful deception, he succeeded in the course of the afternoon in alienating the affections of my only ward. He subsequently stayed to tea, and devoured every single muffin. And what makes his conduct all the more heartless is, that he was perfectly well aware from the first that I have no brother, that I never had a brother, and that I don't intend to have a brother, not even of any kind. I distinctly told him so myself yesterday afternoon.

CYRANO DE BERGERAC
by Edmond Rostand
translated by Gertrude Hall
The Hotel de Bourgogne - 1640 - Cyrano (30-40)

When a boorish fellow comments on the size of his famous proboscis, noble Cyrano illustrates that it is eloquence rather than cheap shots that wins the evening.

CYRANO: *(Imperturbable.)* Is that all?

[VALVERT: But...]

CYRANO: Ah, no, young man, that is not enough! You might have said, dear me, there are a thousand things...varying the tone... For instance...here you are:—Aggressive: "I, monsieur, if I had such a nose, nothing would serve but I must cut it off!" Amicable: "It must be in your way while drinking; you ought to have a special beaker made!" Descriptive: "It is a crag!...a peak!...a promontory! ...A promontory, did I say?...It is a peninsula!" Inquisitive: "What may the office be of that oblong receptacle? Is it an inkhorn or a scissor-case?" Mincing: "Do you so dote on birds, you have, fond as a father, been at pains to fit the little darlings with a roost?" Blunt: "Tell me, monsieur, you, when you smoke, is it possible you blow the vapor through your nose without a neighbor crying, 'The chimney is afire'?" Anxious: "Go with caution, I beseech, lest your head, dragged over by that weight, should drag you over!" Tender: "Have a little sunshade made for it! It might get freckled!" Learned: "None but the beast, monsieur, mentioned by Aristophanes the hippocampelephantocamelos, can have borne beneath his forehead so much cartilage and bone!" Offhand: "What, comrade, is that sort of peg in style? Capital to hang one's hat upon!" Emphatic: "No wind can hope, O lordly nose, to give the whole of you a cold, but the Nor'-Wester!" Dramatic: "It is the Red Sea when it bleeds!" Admiring: "What a sign for a perfumer's shop!" Lyrical: "Art thou a Triton, and is that thy conch?" Simple: "A monument! When is admission free?" Deferent: "Suffer, monsieur, that I should pay you my respects: that is what I call possessing a house of your own!" Rustic: "Hi, boys! Call that a nose? Ye don't

91

gull me! It's either a prize carrot or else a stunted gourd!"
Military: "Level against the cavalry!" Practical: "Will you put it up
for raffle? Indubitably, sir, it will be the feature of the game!" And
finally in parody of weeping Pyramus: "Behold, behold the nose that
traitorously destroyed the beauty of its master! and is blushing for
the same!"—That, my dear sir, or something not unlike, is what you
would have said to me, had you the smallest leaven of letters or of
wit; but of wit, O most pitiable of objects made by God, you never
had a rudiment, and of letters, you have just those that are needed
to spell "fool!"—But, had it been otherwise, and had you been
possessed of the fertile fancy requisite to shower upon me, here, in
this noble company, that volley of sprightly pleasantries, still should
you not have delivered yourself of so much as a quarter of the tenth
part of the beginning of the first....For I let off these good things at
myself, and with sufficient zest, but do not suffer another to let them
off at me!

[DE GUICHE: *(Attempting to lead away the amazed VICOMTE.)*
Let be, Vicomte!]

[VALVERT: That insufferable haughty bearing!...A clodhopper
without...without so much as gloves...who goes abroad without
points...or bow-knots!...]

CYRANO: My foppery is of the inner man. I do not trick myself
out like a popinjay, but I am more fastidious, if I am not so showy.
I would not sally forth, by any chance, not washed quite clean of an
affront; my conscience foggy about the eye, my honor crumpled, my
nicety black-rimmed. I walk with all upon me furbished bright. I
plume myself with independence and straightforwardness. It is not
a handsome figure, it is my soul that I hold erect as in a brace. I go
decked with exploits in place of ribbon bows. I taper to a point my
wit like a mustache. And at my passage through the crowd true
sayings ring like spurs!

[VALVERT: But, sir...]

CYRANO: I am without gloves?...a mighty matter! I only had one
left, of a very ancient pair, and even that became a burden to me...
I left it in somebody's face.

UNCLE VANYA
Scenes from Country Life
by Anton P. Chekhov
translated by Marian Fell
A country estate - 19th century Russia - Astroff (30-40)

Here, a passionate environmentalist chastises Voitski for destroying his forests for wood to burn.

ATSROFF: You can burn peat in your stoves and build your sheds of stone. Oh, I don't object, of course, to cutting wood from necessity, but why destroy the forests? The woods of Russia are trembling under the blows of the axe. Millions of trees have perished. The homes of the wild animals and birds have been desolated, the rivers are shrinking, and many beautiful landscapes are gone forever. And why? Because men are too lazy and stupid to stoop down and pick up their fuel from the ground. *(To HELENA.)* Am I not right, Madame? Who but a stupid barbarian could burn so much beauty in his stove and destroy that which he cannot make? Man is endowed with reason and the power to create so that he may increase that which has been given him but until now he had not created but demolished. The forests are disappearing, the rivers are running dry, the game is exterminated, the climate is spoiled, and the earth becomes poorer and uglier every day. *(To VOITSKI.)* I read irony in your eye; you do not take what I am saying seriously and—and—after all it may very well be nonsense. But when I pass peasant-forests that I have preserved from the axe or hear the rustling of the young plantations set out with my own hands I feel as if I had had some small share in improving the climate and that if mankind is happy a thousand years from now I will have been a little bit responsible for their happiness. When I plant a little birch tree and then see it budding into young green and swaying in the wind, my heart swells with pride and I— *(Sees the WORKMAN, who is bringing him a glass of voldka on a tray.)* However— *(He drinks.)* I must be off. Probably it is all nonsense, anyway. Goodbye.

THE DREAM PLAY
by August Strindberg
translated by Edwin Bjorkman
The legendary Fingal's Cave - The Lawyer (40-60)

This bitter man reveals the sorrow of his life's worth to the
daughter of Indra.

THE LAWYER: *(Goes over to THE DAUGHTER.)* Tell me, sister,
can I have that shawl? I shall keep it here until I have a fire in my
grate, and then I shall burn it with all its miseries and sorrows.
[THE DAUGHTER: Not yet, brother. I want it to hold all it
possibly can, and I want it above all to take up your agonies—all the
confidences you have received about crime, vice, robbery, slander,
abuse—]
THE LAWYER: My dear girl, for such a purpose your shawl
would prove totally insufficient. Look at these walls. Does it not
look as if the wall-paper itself had been soiled by every conceivable
sin? Look at these documents into which I write tales of wrong.
Look at myself— No smiling man ever comes here; nothing is to be
seen here but angry glances, snarling lips, clenched fists— And
everybody pours his anger, his envy, his suspicions, upon me.
Look—my hands are black, and no washing will clean them. See
how they are chapped and bleeding— I can never wear my clothes
more than a few days because they smell of other people's crimes—
At times I have the place fumigated with sulphur, but it does not
help. I sleep near by, and I dream of nothing but crimes— Just
now I have a murder case in court—oh, I can stand that, but do you
know what is worse than anything else?— That is to separate
married people! Then it is as if something cried way down in the
earth and up there in the sky—as if it cried treason against the primal
force, against the source of all good, against love— And do you
know, when reams of paper have been filled with mutual
accusations, and at last a sympathetic person takes one of the two
apart and asks, with a pinch of the ear and a smile, the simple
question: what have you really got against your husband?—or your

94

wife?—then he, or she, stands perplexed and cannot give the cause. Once—well, I think a lettuce salad was the principal issue; another time it was just a word—mostly it is nothing at all. But the tortures, the sufferings—these I have to bear— See how I look! Do you think I could ever win a woman's love with this countenance so like a criminal's? Do you think anybody dares to be friendly with me, who have to collect all the debts, all the money obligations, of the whole city?— It is a misery to be man!

A FLORENTINE TRAGEDY
by Oscar Wilde
A palazzo in Florence - 1900's - Simone (40's)

When Simone and his wife are paid a visit by the son of the
Prince of Florence, he trips over himself to flatter his guest.

SIMONE: My noble Lord, you bring me such high honour that my
tongue like a slave's tongue is tied, and cannot say the word it
would. Yet not to give you thanks were to be too unmannerly. So,
I thank you, from my heart's core. It is such things as these that
knit a state together, when a Prince so nobly born and of such fair
address, forgetting unjust Fortune's differences, comes to an honest
burgher's honest home as a most honest friend. And yet, my Lord,
I fear I am too bold. Some other night we trust that you will come
here as a friend, to-night you come to buy my merchandise. Is it not
so? Silks, velvets, what you will, I doubt not but I have some dainty
wares will woo your fancy. True, the hour is late, but we poor
merchants toil both night and day to make our scanty gains. The
tolls are high, and every city levies its own toll, and prentices are
unskilful, and wives even lack sense and cunning, though Bianca
here has brought me a rich customer to-night. Is it not so, Bianca?
But I waste time. Where is my pack? Where is my pack, I say?
Open it, my good wife. Unloose the cords. Kneel down upon the
floor. You are better so. Nay not that one, the other. Despatch,
despatch! Buyers will grow impatient oftentimes. We dare not keep
them waiting. Ay! 'tis that, give it to me; with care. It is most
costly. Touch it with care. And now, my noble Lord—Nay,
pardon, I have here a Lucca damask, the very web of silver and the
roses so cunningly wrought that they lack perfume merely to cheat
the wanton sense. Touch it, my Lord. Is it not soft as water, strong
as steel? And then the roses! Are they not finely woven? I think
the hillsides that best love the rose, at Bellosguardo or at Fiesole,
throw no such blossoms on the lap of spring, or if they do their
blossoms droop and die. Such is the fate of all the dainty things that
dance in wind and water. Nature herself makes war on her own

loveliness and slays her children like Medea. Nay but, my Lord, look closer still. Why in this damask here it is summer always, and no winter's tooth will ever blight these blossoms. For every ell I paid a piece of gold. Red gold, and good, the fruit of careful thrift.

THE GLITTERING GATE
by Lord Dunsany
A lonely place - Bill (Any age)

Bill and Jim find themselves standing outside a large gate that they assume is the entrance to Heaven. As Bill tries to pry the gate open, he shares his vision of paradise with Jim.

BILL: Can't be, Jim. These doors are meant to open outward. They couldn't do that if they were more than four inches at the most, not for an Archbishop. They'd stick.

[JIM: You remember that great safe we broke open once, what had coal in it.]

BILL: This isn't a safe, Jim, this is Heaven. There'll be old saints with their halos shining and flickering, like windows o' wintry nights. *(Creak, creak, creak.)* And angels thick as swallows along a cottage roof the day before they go. *(Creak, creak, creak.)* And orchards full of apples as far as you can see, and the rivers of Tigris and Euphrates, so the Bible says; and a city of gold, for those that care for cities, all full of precious stones; but I'm a bit tired of cities and precious stones. *(Creak, creak, creak.)* I'll go out into the fields where the orchards are, by the Tigris and the Euphrates. I shouldn't be surprised if my old mother was there. She never cared much for the way I earned my livelihood *(creak, creak)*, but she was a good mother to me. I don't know if they want a good mother in there who would be kind to the angels and sit and smile at them when they sang and soothe them if they were cross. If they let all the good ones in she'll be there all right. *(Suddenly.)* Jim! They won't have brought me up against her, will they? That's not fair evidence, Jim.

[JIM: It would be just like them to. Very like them.]

BILL: If there's a glass of beer to be got in Heaven, or a dish of tripe and onions, or a pipe of 'bacca she'll have them for me when I come to her. She used to know my ways wonderful; and what I liked. And she used to know when to expect me almost anywhere. I used to climb in through the window at any hour and she always knew it was me. *(Creak, creak.)* She'll know it's me at the door now, Jim. *(Creak, creak.)* It will be all a blaze of light, and I'll hardly know it's here till I get used to it...But I'll know her among a million angels. There weren't none like her on Earth and there won't be none like her in Heaven...Jim! I'm through, Jim! One more turn, and "Old Nut-cracker"'s done it! It's giving! It's giving! I know the feel of it. *Jim!*

THE PASSION FLOWER
by Jacinto Benavente
translated by John Garrett Underhill
A farmhouse in Castille - 1920's - Esteban (40-50)

Esteban has fallen in love with his wife's daughter by her first
husband and has murdered the young woman's fiance in a
jealous rage. When his wife confronts him with his evil deeds,
he tries to explain.

ESTEBAN: Raimunda! Wife! Pity me! You don't know. Don't
talk to me. No, I am the one who must talk—I must confess as I
shall confess at the hour of my doom! You don't know how I have
struggled. I have wrestled all these years as with another man who
was stronger than I, night and day, who was dragging me where I
did not want to go.
[RAIMUNDA: But when—when did that evil thought first enter
your mind? When was that unhappy hour?]
ESTEBAN: [I don't know.] It came upon me like a blight, all at
once; it was there. All of us think some evil in our lives, but the
thought passes away, it does not harm; it is gone. When I was a
boy, one day my father beat me. Quick as a flash it came to me: "I
wish he was dead!" But no sooner thought, than I was ashamed—I
was ashamed to think that I had ever had such a thought. My heart
stood still within me for fear that God had heard, that He would take
him away. From that day I love him more, and when he died, years
afterward, I grieved as much for that thought as I did for his death,
although I was a grown man. And this might have been the same;
but this did not go away. I became more fixed the more I struggled
to shake it off. You can't say that I did not love you. I loved you
more every day! You can't say that I cast my eyes on other
women—and I had no thought of her. But when I felt her by me my
blood took fire. When we sat down to eat, I was afraid to look up.
Wherever I turned she was there, before me—always! At night,
when we were in bed, and I was lying close to you in the midnight
silence of the house, all I could feel was her. I could hear her

breathe as if her lips had been at my ear. I wept for spite, for bitterness! I prayed to God, I scourged myself. I could have killed myself—and her! Words cannot tell the horror I went through. The few times that we were alone, I ran from her like a wild man. If I had stayed I don't know what might have happened: I might have kissed her, I might have dug my knife into her!

THE HAIRY APE
by Eugene O'Neill
An ocean liner - 1 hour after leaving New York - Paddy (50-60)

As the hands gather to drink and gossip, the senior member of their ranks reminisces about days gone by.

PADDY: *(Who has been sitting in a blinking, melancholy daze—suddenly cries out in a voice full of old sorrow.)* We belong to this, you're saying? We make the ship to go, you're saying? Yerra then, that Almighty God have pity on us! *(His voice runs into the wail of a keen; he rocks back and forth on his bench. The men stare at him, startled and impressed in spite of themselves.)* Oh, to be back in the fine days of my youth, ochone! Oh, there was fine beautiful ships them days—clippers wid tall masts touching the sky—fine strong men in them—men that was sons of the sea as if 'twas the mother that bore them. Oh, the clean skins of them, and the clear eyes, the straight backs and full chests of them! Brave men they was, and bold men surely! We'd be sailing out, bound down round the Horn maybe. We'd be making sail in the dawn, no care to it. And astern the land would be sinking low and dying out, but we'd give it no heed but a laugh, and never a look behind. For the day that was, was enough, for we was free men—and I'm thinking 'tis only slaves do be giving heed to the day that's gone or the day to come—until they're old like me. *(With a sort of religious exaltation.)* Oh, to be scudding south again wid the power of the Trade Wind driving her on steady through the nights and the days! Nights when the foam of the wake would be flaming wid fire, when the sky'd be blazing and winking wid stars. Or the full of the moon maybe. Then you'd see her driving through the gray night, her sails stretching aloft all silver and white, not a sound on the deck, the lot of us dreaming dreams, till you'd believe 'twas no real ship at all you was on but a ghost ship like the *Flying Dutchman* they says does be roaming the seas forevermore widout touching a port. And there was the days, too. A warm sun on the clean decks. Sun warming the blood of you, and wind over the miles of shiny green ocean like

102

strong drink to your lungs. Work—aye, hard work—but who'd mind that at all? Sure, you worked under the sky and 'twas work wid skill and daring to it. And wid the day done, in the dog watch, smoking me pipe at ease, the lookout would be raising land maybe, and we'd see the mountains of South Americy wid red fire of the setting sun painting their white tops and the clouds floating by them! *(His tone of exaltation ceases. He goes on mournfully.)* Yerra, what's the use of talking? 'Tis a dead man's whisper. *(To YANK resentfully.)* 'Twas them days a ship was part of the sea, and a man was part of a ship, and the sea joined all together and made it one. *(Scornfully.)* Is it one wid this you'd be, Yank—black smoke from the funnels smudging the sea, smudging the decks—the bloody engines pounding and throbbing and shaking—wid divil a sight of sun or a breath of clean air—choking our lungs wid coal dust— breaking our backs and hearts in the hell of the stokehole—feeding the bloody furnace—feeding our lives along wid the coal, I'm thinking—caged in by steel from a sight of the sky like bloody apes in the zoo! *(With a harsh laugh.)* Ho-ho, divil mend you! Is it to belong to that you're wishing? It is a flesh and blood wheel of the engines you'd be?

THE ADDING MACHINE
by Elmer Rice
An unspecified city - 1920's - Mr. Zero (45-50)

When he is arrested and tried for murder, Mr. Zero addresses the jury with the sad state of his life.

ZERO: *(Beginning to speak haltingly)* Sure I killed him. I ain't sayin' I didn't, am I? Sure I killed him. Them lawyers give me a good stiff pain, that's what they give me. Half the time I don't know what the hell they're talkin' about. Objection sustained. Objection over-ruled. What's the big idea, anyhow? You ain't heard me do any objectin', have you? Sure not! What's the idea of objectin'? You got a right to know. What I say is if one bird kills another bird, why you got a right to call him for it. That's what I say. I know all about that. I been on a jury, too. Them lawyers! Don't let 'em fill you full of bunk. All that bull about it bein' red ink on the bill-file. Red ink nothin'! It was blood, see? I want you to get that right. I killed him, see? Right through the heart with the bill-file, see? I want you to get that right—all of you. One, two, three, four, five, six, seven, eight, nine, ten, eleven, twelve. Twelve of you. Six and six. That makes twelve. I figgered it up often enough. Six and six makes twelve. And five is seventeen. And eight is twenty-five. And three is twenty-eight. Eight and carry two. Aw, cut it out! Them damn figgers! I can't forget 'em. Twenty-five years, see? Eight hours a day, exceptin' Sundays. And July and August half-day Saturday. One week's vacation with pay. And another week without pay if you want it. Who the hell wants it? Layin' around the house listenin' to the wife tellin' you where you get off. Nix! An' legal holidays. I nearly forget them. New Year's, Washington's Birthday, Decoration Day, Fourth o' July, Labor Day, Thanksgivin', Christmas. Good Friday if you want it. An' if you're a Jew, Young Kipper an' the other one—I forgot what they call it. The dirty sheenies—always gettin' two to the other bird's one. And when a holiday comes on Sunday, you get Monday off. So that's fair enough. But when the Fourth o' July comes on

104

THE ADDING MACHINE

Saturday, why you're out o' luck on account of Saturday bein' a half-day anyhow. Get me? Twenty-five years—I'll tell you somethin' funny. Decoration Day an' the Fourth o' July are always on the same day o' the week. Twenty-five years. Never missed a day, and never more'n five minutes late. Look at my time card if you don't believe me. Eight twenty-seven, eight thirty, eight twenty-nine, eight twenty-seven, eight thirty-two. Eight an' thirty-two's forty an'—Goddam them figgers! I can't forget 'em. They're funny things, them figgers. They look like people sometimes. The eights, see? Two dots for eyes and a dot for the nose. An' a line. That's the mouth, see? An' there's others remind you of other things—but I can't talk about them on account of there bein' ladies here. Sure I killed him. Why didn't he shut up? If he'd only shut up! Instead o' talkin' an' talkin' about how sorry he was an' what a good guy I was an' this an' that. I felt like sayin' to him: "For Christ's sake, shut up!" But I didn't have the nerve, see? I didn't have the nerve to say that to the boss. An' he went on talkin', sayin' how sorry he was, see? He was standin' right close to me. An' his coat only had two buttons on it. Two an' two makes four an'—aw, can it! An' there was the bill-file on the desk. Right where I could touch it. It ain't right to kill a guy. I know that. When I read all about him in the paper an' about his three kids I felt like a cheap skate, I tell you. They had the kids' pictures in the paper, right next to mine. An' his wife, too. Gee, it must be swell to have a wife like that. Some guys sure is lucky. An' he left fifty thousand dollars just for a rest-room for the girls in the store. He was a good guy, at that. Fifty thousand. That's more'n twice as much as I'd have if I saved every nickel I ever made. Let's see. Twenty-five an' twenty-five an' twenty-five an'—aw, cut it out! An' the ads had a big, black border around 'em; an' all it said was that the store would be closed for three days on account of the boss bein' dead. That nearly handed me a laugh, that did. All them floor-walkers an' buyers an' high-muck-a-mucks havin' me to thank for gettin' three days off. I hadn't oughta killed him. I ain't sayin' nothin' about that. But I thought he was goin' to give me a raise, see? On account of bein' there twenty-five years. He never talked to me before, see? Except one mornin' we happened to come in the store together and I held the door open for him and he said "Thanks." Just like that, see? "Thanks!" That was the only time he ever talked to me. An' when I seen him comin' up to my desk, I didn't know where I got off. A big guy like that comin' up to my desk. I felt like I was chokin' like and all of a sudden I got a kind o' bad taste in my mouth like when you get up in the mornin'. I didn't have no right to kill him. The district attorney is right about that. He read the law to you, right out o' the book. Killin' a bird—that's wrong. But there was that girl, see? Six months they gave her. It was a dirty trick tellin' the cops on her like that. I shouldn't 'a' done that. But what was I gonna do? The wife wouldn't let up on me. I hadda do it. She used to walk around the room, just in her undershirt, see? Nothin' else on. Just her undershirt. An' they gave her six months. That's the last I'll ever see of her. Them birds—how do they get away with it? Just grabbin' women, they way you see 'em do in the pictures. I've seen lots I'd like to grab like that, but I ain't got the nerve—in the subway an' on the street an' in the store buyin' things. Pretty soft for them shoe-salesmen, I'll say, lookin' at women's legs all day. Them lawyers! They give me a pain, I tell you—a pain! Sayin' the same thing over an' over again. I never said I didn't kill him. But that ain't the same as bein' a regular murderer. What good did it do me to kill him? I didn't make nothin' out of it. Answer yes or no! Yes or no, me elbow! There's some things you can't answer yes or no. Give me the once-over, you guys. Do I look like a murderer? Do I? I never did no harm to nobody. Ask the wife. She'll tell you. Ask anybody. I never got into trouble. You wouldn't count that one time at the Polo Grounds. That was just fun like. Everybody was yellin', "Kill the empire! Kill the empire!" An' before I knew what I was doin' I fired the pop bottle. It was on account of everybody yellin' like that. Just in fun like, see? The yeller dog! Callin' that one a strike—a mile away from the plate. Anyhow, the bottle didn't hit him. An' when I seen the cop comin' up the aisle, I beat it. That didn't hurt nobody. It was just in fun like, see? An' that time in the subway. I was readin' about a lynchin', see? Down in Georgia. They took the nigger an' they tied him to a tree. An' they poured kerosene on him and lit a big fire under him. The dirty nigger! Boy, I'd of liked to been there, with a gat in each hand pumpin' him full of lead. I was readin' about it in the subway, see? Right at Times Square where the big crowd gets on. An' all of a sudden this big nigger steps right on my foot. It was lucky for him I didn't have a gun on me. I'd of killed him sure, I guess. I guess he couldn't help it all right on account of the crowd, but a nigger's got no right to step on a white man's foot. I told him where he got off all right. The dirty nigger. But that didn't hurt nobody, either. I'm a pretty steady guy, you gotta admit that. Twenty-five years in one job an' I never missed a day. Fifty-two weeks in a year. Fifty-two an' fifty-two an' fifty two an'—They didn't have t' look for me, did they? I didn't try to run away, did I? Where was I goin' to run to! I wasn't thinkin' about it at all, see? I'll tell you what I was thinkin' about— how I was goin' to break it to the wife about bein' canned. He canned me after twenty-five years, see? Did the lawyers tell you about that? I forget. All that talk gives me a headache. Objection sustained. Objection over-ruled. Answer yes or no. It gives me a headache. And I can't get the figgers outta my head, neither. But that's what I was thinkin' about—how I was goin' t' break it to the wife about bein' canned. An' what Miss Devore would think when she heard about me killin' him. I bet she never thought I had the nerve to do it. I'd of married her if the wife had passed out. I'd be holdin' down my job yet, if he hadn't o' canned me. But he kept talkin' an' talkin'. An' there was the bill-file right where I could reach it. Do you get me? I'm just a regular guy like anybody else. Like you birds, now.

HENRY IV
by Luigi Pirandello
translated by Edward Storer
A solitary villa in Italy in our own time - Henry IV (50)

A wealthy madman who has assumed the identity of
Shakespeare's Henry IV here rants at his servants.

HENRY IV: *(Answers them imperiously.)* Enough! enough! Let's
stop it. I'm tired of it. *(Then as if the thought left him no peace.)*
By God! The impudence! To come here along with her lover!...
And pretending to do it out of pity! So as not to infuriate a poor
devil already out of the world, out of time, out of life! If it hadn't
been supposed to be done out of pity, one can well imagine that
fellow wouldn't have allowed it. Those people expect others to
behave as they wish all the time. And, of course, there's nothing
arrogant in that! Oh, no! Oh, no! It's merely their way of
thinking, of feeling, of seeing. Everybody has his own way of
thinking; you fellows, too. Yours is that of a flock of sheep—
miserable, feeble, uncertain...But those others take advantage of this
and make you accept their way of thinking; or, at least, they suppose
they do; because, after all, what do they succeed in imposing on
you? Words, words which anyone can interpret in his own manner!
That's the way public opinion is formed! And it's a bad lookout for
a man who finds himself labeled one day with one of these words
which everyone repeats; for example "madman," or "imbecile."
Don't you think it rather hard for a man to keep quiet, when he
knows that there is a fellow going about trying to persuade everybody that he is as he sees him, trying to fix him in other people's
opinion as a "madman"—according to him? Now I am talking
seriously! Before I hurt my head, falling from my horse... *(Stops
suddenly, noticing the dismay of the four YOUNG MEN.)* What's the
matter with you? *(Imitates their amazed looks.)* What? Am I, or
am I not, mad? Oh, yes! I'm mad all right! *(He becomes terrible.)*
Well then, by God, down on your knees, down on your knees!
(Makes them go down on their knees one by one.) I order you to go

down on your knees before me! And touch the ground three times with your foreheads! Down, down! That's the way you've got to be before madmen! *(Then annoyed with their facile humiliation.)* Get up, sheep! You obeyed me, didn't you? You might have put the strait jacket on me!...Crush a man with the weight of a word—it's nothing—a fly! all our life is crushed by the weight of words: the weight of the dead. Look at me here: can you really suppose that Henry IV is still alive? All the same, I speak, and order you live men about! Do you think it's a joke that the dead continue to live?—Yes, *here* it's a joke! But get out into the live world!—Ah, you say: what a beautiful sunrise—for us! All time is before us!—Dawn! We will do what we like with this day.—Ah, yes! To Hell with tradition, the old conventions! Well, go on! You will do nothing but repeat the old, old words, while you imagine you are living! *(Goes up to BERTHOLD, who has now become quite stupid.)* You don't understand a word of this, do you?

HENRY IV
by Luigi Pirandello
translated by Edward Storer

A solitary villa in Italy in our own time - Henry IV (50)
Here, Henry offers a fascinating treatise on madness.

HENRY IV: Your being so dismayed because now I seem again mad to you. You have thought me mad up to now, haven't you? You feel that this dismay of yours can become terror too—something to dash away the ground from under your feet and deprive you of the air you breathe! Do you know what it means to find yourselves face to face with a madman—with one who shakes the foundations of all you have built up in yourselves, your logic, or rather with a logic that flies like a feather. Voluble! Voluble! Today like this and tomorrow—who knows? You say: "This cannot be"; but for them everything can be. You say: "This isn't true!" And why? Because it doesn't seem true to you, or you, or you...*(Indicates the three of them in succession.)*...and to a hundred thousand others! One must see what seems true to these hundred thousand others who are not supposed to be mad! What a magnificent spectacle they afford when they reason! What flowers of logic they scatter! I know that when I was a child, I thought the moon in the pond was real. How many things I thought real! I believed everything I was told—and I was happy! Because it's a terrible thing if you don't hold on to that which seems true to you today—to that which will seem true to you tomorrow, even if it is the opposite of that which seemed true to you yesterday. I would never wish you to think, as I have done, on this horrible thing which really drives one mad: that if you were beside another and looking into his eyes—as I one day looked into somebody's eyes—you might as well be a beggar before a door never to be opened to you; for he who does enter there will never be you, but someone unknown to you with hisown different and impenetrable world...*(Long Pause. Darkness gathers in the room, increasing the sense of strangeness and consternation in which the four YOUNG MEN are involved. HENRY IV remains aloof, pondering on the misery which is not only his, but everybody's. Then he pulls himself up, and says in an ordinary tone.)* It's getting dark here...

110

DESIRE UNDER THE ELMS
by Eugene O'Neill
The Cabot farmhouse in New England - 1850 - Ephraim Cabot (70)

Ephraim's young wife has been unable to conceive the son he desires to inherit his farm. Here, Ephraim tells her the story of his battle to carve out his own life and his need for an heir.

CABOT: *(suddenly raises his head and looks at her—scornfully)* Will ye ever know me—'r will any man 'r woman? *(shaking his head)* No. I calc'late 't wa'n't t' be. *(He turns away. ABBIE looks at the wall. Then, evidently unable to keep silent about his thoughts, without looking at his wife, he puts out his hand and clutches her knee. She starts violently, looks at him, sees he is not watching her, concentrates again on the wall and pays no attention to what he says.)* Listen, Abbie. When I come here fifty odd year ago—I was jest twenty an' the strongest an' hardest ye ever seen—ten times as strong an' fifty times as hard as Eben. Waal—this place was nothin' but fields o' stones. Folks laughed when I tuk it. They couldn't know what I knowed. When ye kin make corn sprout out o' stones, God's livin' in yew! They wa'n't strong enuf fur that! They reckoned God was easy. They laughed. They don't laugh no more. Some died hereabouts. Some went West an' died. They're all under ground—fur follerin' arter an easy God. God hain't easy. *(He shakes his head slowly)* An' I growed hard. Folks kept allus sayin' he's a hard man like 'twas sinful t' be hard, so's at last I said back at 'em: Waal then, by thunder, ye'll git me hard an' see how ye like it! *(then suddenly)* But I give in t' weakness once. 'Twas arter I'd been here two year. I got weak—despairful—they was so many stones. They was a party leavin', givin' up, goin' West. I jined 'em. We tracked on 'n on. We come t' broad medders, lains, whar the soil was black an 'rich as gold. Nary a stone. Easy. Ye'd on'y to plow an' sow an' then set an 'smoke yer pipe an' watch thin's grow. I could o' been a rich man—but somethin' in me fit me an' fit me—the voice o' God sayin': "This hain't wuth nothin' t' Me. Get ye back t' hum!" I got afeerd o' that voice an' I lit out back t'

111

hum here, leavin' my claim an' crops t' whoever'd a mind t' take 'em. Ay-eh. I actoolly give up what was rightful mine! God's hard, not easy! God's in the stones! Build my church on a rock— out o' stones an' I'll be in them! That's what He meant t' Peter! *(He sighs heavily—a pause)* Stones. I picked 'em up an' piled 'em into walls. Ye kin read the years o' my life in them walls every day a hefted stone, climbin' over the hills up and down, fencin' in the fields that was mine, whar I'd made thin's grow out o' nothin'—like the will o' God, like the servant o' His hand. It wa'n't easy. It was hard an' He made me hard fur it. *(He pauses)* All the time I kept gittin' lonesomer. I tuk a wife. She bore Simeon an' Peter. She was a good woman. She wuked hard. We was married twenty year. She never knowed me. She helped but she never knowed what she was helpin'. I was allus lonesome. She died. After that it wa'n't so lonesome fur a spell. *(a pause)* I lost count o' the years. I had no time t' fool away countin' 'em. Sim an' Peter helped. The farm growed. It was all mine! When I thought o' that I didn't feel lonesome. *(a pause)* But ye can't hitch yer mind t' one thin' day an' night. I tuk another wife—Eben's Maw. Her folks was contestin' me at law over my deeds t' the farm—my farm! That's why Eben keeps a-talkin' his fool talk o' this bein' his Maw's farm. She bore Eben. She was purty—but soft. She tried t' be hard. She couldn't. She never knowed me nor nothin'. It was lonesomer 'n hell with her. After a matter o' sixteen odd years, she died. *(a pause)* I lived with the boys. They hated me 'cause I was hard. I hated them 'cause they was soft. They coveted the farm without knowin' what it meant. It made me bitter 'n wormwood. It aged me—them coveting what I'd made fur mine. Then this spring the call come—the voice o' God cryin' in my wilderness, in my lonesomeness—t' go out an' seek an' find! *(turning to her with strange passion)* I sought ye an' I found ye! Yew air my Rose o' Sharon! Yer eyes air like.... *(She has turned a blank face, resentful eyes to his. He stares at her for a moment—then harshly)* Air ye any the wiser fur all I've told ye?

THE DEVIL AND DANIEL WEBSTER
by Stephen Vincent Benet
Cross Corners, NH - 1841 - Mr. Scratch (30-60)

Here, the clever Mr. Scratch summons the jury of the damned
to sit in judgement on Mr. Stone.

SCRATCH: The quick or the dead! You have said it! *(He points
his finger at the place where the jury is to appear. There is a clap
of thunder and a flash of light. The stage blacks out completely. All
that can be seen is the face of SCRATCH, lit with a ghastly green
light as he recites the invocation that summons the JURY. As, one
by one, the important JURYMEN are mentioned, they appear.)*
        I summon the jury Mr. Webster demands.
        From churchyard mould and gallows grave,
        Brimstone pit and burning gulf,
        I summon them!
        Dastard, liar, scoundrel, knave,
        I summon them! Appear!
        There's Simon Girty, the renegade,
        The haunter of the forest glade
        Who joined with Indian and wolf
        To hunt the pioneer.
        The stains upon his hunting-shirt
        Are not the blood of the deer.
        There's Walter Butler, the loyalist,
        Who carried a firebrand in his fist
        Of massacre and shame.
        King Philip's eye is wild and bright.
        They slew him in the great Swamp Fight,
        But still, with terror and affright,
        The land recalls his name.
        Blackbeard Teach, the pirate fell,
        Smeet the strangler, hot from hell,
        Dale, who broke men on the wheel,
        Morton, of the tarnished steel,

THE DEVIL AND DANIEL WEBSTER

I summon them, I summon them
From their tormented flame!
Quick or dead, quick or dead,
Broken heart and bitter head,
True Americans, each one,
Traitor and disloyal son,
Cankered earth and twisted tree,
Outcasts of eternity,
Twelve great sinners, tried and true,
For the work they are to do!
I summon them, I summon them!
Appear, appear, appear!

DEATH OF A SALESMAN
by Arthur Miller
The Loman house, 1940's - Willy Loman (50-60)

Willy Loman has spent his life on the road. The realization that his children have grown up without him, combined with his growing disenchantment with the traveling life, lead's Willy to make the following desperate plea to his boss.

WILLY: *(angrily).* Business is definitely business, but just listen for a minute. You don't understand this. When I was a boy— eighteen, nineteen—I was already on the road. And there was a question in my mind as to whether selling had a future for me. Because in those days I had a yearning to go to Alaska. See, there were three gold strikes in one month in Alaska, and I felt like going out. Just for the ride, you might say.

[HOWARD: *(barely interested).* Don't say.]

WILLY: Oh, yeah, my father lived many years in Alaska. He was an adventurous man. We've got quite a little streak of self-reliance in our family. I thought I'd go out with my older brother and try to locate him, and maybe settle in the North with the old man. And I was almost decided to go, when I met a salesman in the Parker House. His name was Dave Singleman. And he was eighty-four years old, and he'd drummed merchandise in thirty-one states. And old Dave, he'd go up to his room, y'understand, put on his green velvet slippers—I'll never forget—and pick up his phone and call the buyers, and without ever leaving his room, at the age of eighty-four, he made his living. And when I saw that, I realized that selling was the greatest career a man could want. 'Cause what could be more satisfying than to be able to go, at the age of eighty-four, into twenty or thirty different cities, and pick up a phone, and be remembered and loved and helped by so many different people? Do you know? when he died—and by the way he died the death of a salesman, in his green velvet slippers in the smoker of the New York, New Haven, and Hartford, going into Boston—when he died, hundreds of salesmen and buyers were at his funeral. Things were said on a lotta trains for months after that. *(He stands up. HOWARD has not looked at him.)* In those days there was personality in it, Howard. There was respect, and comradeship, and gratitude in it. Today, it's all cut and dried, and there's no chance for bringing friendship to bear—or personality. You see what I mean? They don't know me any more.

CAMINO REAL
by Tennessee Williams

A fantasy limbo called "Camino Real" - Lord Byron (40's)

Here, Lord Byron describes the cremation of Percy Shelley.

BYRON: When Shelley's corpse was recovered from the sea... *(GUTMAN beckons the DREAMER who approaches and accompanies BYRON'S speech.)*—It was burned on the beach at Viareggio.—I watched the spectacle from my carriage because the stench was revolting...Then it—fascinated me! I got out of my carriage. Went nearer, holding a handkerchief to my nostrils!—I saw that the front of the skull had broken away in the flames, and there— *(He advances out upon the stage apron, followed by ABDULLAH with the pine torch or lantern.)* And there was the brain of Shelley, indistinguishable from a cooking stew!—*boiling, bubbling, hissing!*—in the *blackening—cracked—pot*—of his skull! *(MARGUERITE rises abruptly. JACQUES supports her.)*— Trelawney, his friend, Trelawney, threw salt and oil and frankincense in the flames and finally the almost intolerable stench— *(ABDULLAH giggles. GUTMAN slaps him.]* —was *gone* and the burning was *pure!*—as a man's burning should be...

A man's burning *ought* to be pure!—*not* like mine—(a crepe suzette—burned in brandy...)

Shelley's burning was finally very *pure!*

But the body, the corpse, split open like a grilled pig! *(ABDULLAH giggles irrepressibly again. GUTMAN grips the back of his neck and he stands up stiff and assumes an expression of exaggerated solemnity.)* —And then Trelawney—as the ribs of the corpse unlocked— reached into them as a baker reaches quickly into an oven! *(ABDULLAH almost goes into another convulsion.)* —And snatched out—as a baker would a biscuit!—the *heart* of Shelley! Snatched the heart of Shelley out of the blistering corpse!—Out of the purifying— blue-flame... *(MARGUERITE resumes her seat; JACQUES his.)* —And it was *over!*—I thought— *(He turns slightly from the audience and crosses upstage from the apron. He faces JACQUES and MARGUERITE.)* —I thought it was a disgusting thing to do, to snatch a man's heart from his body! What can one man do with another man's heart?

117

CAMINO REAL
by Tennessee Williams
A fantasy limbo called "Camino Real" - Lord Byron (40's)

The above dissertation moves Byron to ruminate on the loss of his heart's innocence.

BYRON: That's very true, Señor. But a poet's vocation, which used to be my vocation, is to influence the heart in a gentler fashion than you have made your mark on that loaf of bread. He ought to purify it and lift it above its ordinary level. For what is the heart but a sort of—*(He makes a high, groping gesture in the air.]*—A sort of—*instrument!*—that translates *noise* into *music*, chaos into—*order...* *(ABDULLAH ducks almost to the earth in an effort to stifle his mirth. GUTMAN coughs to cover his own amusement.)*—a mysterious order! *(He raises his voice till it fills the plaza.]*—That was my vocation once upon a time, before it was obscured by vulgar plaudits!—Little by little it was lost among gondolas and palazzos!—masked balls, glittering salons, huge shadowy courts and torch-lit entrances!—Baroque fascades, canopia and carpets, candelabra and gold plate among snowy damask, ladies with throats as slender as flower-stems, bending and breathing toward me their fragrant breath—

—Exposing their breasts to me!

Whispering half-smiling!—And everywhere marble, the visible grandeur of marble, pink and gray marble, veined and tinted as flayed corrupting flesh,—all these provided agreeable distractions from the rather frightening solitude of a poet. Oh, I wrote many cantos in Venice and Constantinople and in Ravenna and Rome, on all of those Latin and Levantine excursions that my twisted foot led me into—but I wonder about them a little. They seem to improve as the wine in the bottle—dwindles...*There is a passion for declivity in this world!*

And lately I've found myself listening to hired musicians behind a row of artificial palm trees—instead of the single—pure-stringed instrument of my heart...

118

Well, then, it's time to leave here! *(He turns back to the stage.)* —There is a time for departure even when there's no certain place to go!

I'm going to look for one, now. I'm sailing to Athens. At least I can look up at the Acropolis, I can stand at the foot of it and look up at broken columns on the crest of a hill—if not purity, at least its recollection...

I can sit quietly looking for a long, long time in absolute silence, and possibly, yes, *still* possibly—

The old pure music will come to me again. Of course on the other hand I may hear only the little noise of insects in the grass...

But I am sailing to Athens! *Make voyages!—Attempt them!*—there's nothing else...

A HAT FULL OF RAIN
by Michael Vincente Gazzo
Lower east side of Manhattan - 1950's - Johnny (20-30)

When his father comes to visit, Johnny is filled with memories
of his childhood, which he here shares with his wife.

JOHNNY: This morning you said that the marriage was a bust, that
we were on the rocks...After you left...Did you ever feel like you
were going crazy? Ever since I knew the old man was coming up...I
just can't stop remembering things...like all night long I've been
hearing that whistle...The old man used to whistle like that when he
used to call us...I was supposed to come right home from school, but
I played marbles. Maybe every half-hour he'd whistle...I'd be on
my knees in the schoolyard, with my immie glove on—you take a
woman's glove and you cut off the fingers...so your fingers are free
and your knuckles don't bleed in the wintertime...and I just kept on
playing and the whistle got madder and madder. It starts to get dark
and I'd get worried but I wouldn't go home until I won all the
marbles...and he'd be up on that porch whistling away. I'd cross
myself at the door...and there was a grandmother I had who taught
me to cross myself to protect myself from lightning...I'd open the
door and go in...hold up the chamois bag of marbles and I'd say,
hey, Pop, I won! Wham! Pow!...I'd wind up in the corner saying,
Pop, I didn't hear you. I didn't hear you...
[CELIA: What did you do today? You didn't play marbles today,
did you? You weren't home all day because I called here five times
if I called once...]
JOHNNY: I'm trying to tell you what I did today...
[CELIA: You're trying to avoid telling me what you did today.]
JOHNNY: I took a train see...then I took a bus...I went to look at
the house I was born in. It's only an hour away...but in fifteen
years, I've never gone anywhere near that house...or that town! I
had to go back...I can't explain the feeling, but I was ten years old
when I left there...The way I looked around, they must have thought
I was crazy...because I kept staring at the old house—I was going to

120

knock at the door and ask the people if I could just look around...
and then I went to that Saybrook school where I used to hear the old
man whistle...and those orange fire escapes...and ivy still climbing
up the walls. Then I took the bus and the train, and I went to meet
the old man's plane...and we came here.

THE CHINESE WALL
by Max Frisch
translated by James L. Rosenberg
The Great Wall of China - Don Juan (30-40)

Don Juan here speaks to Christopher Columbus about the golden
age of discovery and of mankind's desperate need for new
horizons.

DON JUAN: You see: it's a dance of death. Didn't I say so? We
are lost, Captain, if we don't get there.
[COLUMBUS: Where?]
DON JUAN: When I think of your world: Marco Polo, who
discovered China, and it was as though he had arrived on the other
side of time and space; Vasco da Gama; and you—ah, that was a
world open in all directions, surrounded by mystery. There were is-
lands which no human had ever set foot on, continents undiscovered
by man, coasts of hope. A twig floating upon the sea was a twig of
promise. Anything was possible, and everything; the earth was like
a bride. There was poverty, too, I know, injustice, hunger, the
tyranny of kings, but also (and as a result): Hope! There were fruits
which belonged to no man, Paradise which was not yet lost—an
answer to my longing. The Unknown was still possible; adventure
was in the air. A virginal world. And the earth was not what it is
today: a globe cut up into sections once and for all, a big ball that
sits at one's elbow upon the writing desk, complete, contained,
devoid of hope! For man is everywhere, and everything that we
have now discovered has served to make the world, not greater, but
smaller....Let's fly, Captain! In seven days (or four, or less—I don't
know any more) we can circle the entire world, and all those spaces
that represented Hope to you will become transmuted into time,
which we no longer need, for we—we have no more hope, we have
no Beyond!—if you don't give it back to us, Captain.

ENDGAME
by Samuel Beckett
translated by Samuel Beckett
A bare interior - Hamm (40-50)

As Hamm's sense of reality disintegrates, he rambles endlessly
about the weather, corn and porridge.

HAMM: One! Silence! *(pause)* Where was I? *(Pause. Gloomily)*
It's finished, we're finished. *(pause)* Nearly finished. *(pause)*
There'll be no more speech. *(pause)* Something dripping in my
head, ever since the fontanelles. *(stifled hilarity of NAGG)* Splash,
splash, always on the same spot. *(pause)* Perhaps it's a little vein.
(pause) A little artery. *(Pause. More animated)* Enough of that,
it's story time, where was I? *(Pause. Narrative tone)* The man
came crawling towards me, on his belly. Pale, wonderfully pale and
thin, he seemed on the point of— *(Pause. Normal tone)* No. I've
done that bit. *(Pause. Narrative tone)* I calmly filled my pipe—the
meerschaum, lit it with...let us say a vesta, drew a few puffs. Aah!
(pause) Well, what is it you want? *(pause)* It was an extra-
ordinarily bitter day, I remember, zero by the thermometer. But
considering it was Christmas Eve there was nothing...extraordinary
about that. Seasonable weather, for once in a way. *(pause)* Well,
what ill wind blows you my way? He raised his face to me, black
with mingled dirt and tears. *(Pause. Normal tone)* That should do
it. *(narrative tone)* No no, don't look at me, don't look at me. He
dropped his eyes and mumbled something, apologies I presume.
(pause) I'm a busy man, you know, the final touches, before the
festivities, you know what it is. *(Pause. Forcibly)* Come on now,
what is the object of this invasion? *(pause)* It was a glorious bright
day, I remember, fifty by the heliometer, but already the sun was
sinking down into the...down among the dead. *(normal tone)*
Nicely put, that. *(narrative tone)* Come on now, come on, present
your petition and let me resume my labors. *(Pause. Normal tone)*
There's English for you. Ah well... *(narrative tone)* It was then
he took the plunge. It's my little one, he said. Tsstss, a little one,

that's bad. My little boy, he said, as if the sex mattered. Where did he come from? He named the hole. A good half-day, on horse. What are you insinuating? That the place is still inhabited? No no, not a soul, except himself and the child—assuming he existed. Good. I inquired about the situation at Kov, beyond the gulf. Not a sinner. Good. And you expect me to believe you have left your little one back there, all alone, and alive into the bargain? Come now! *(pause)* It was a howling wild day, I remember, a hundred by the anenometer. The wind was tearing up the dead pines and sweeping them...away. *(Pause. Normal tone)* A bit feeble, that. *(narrative tone)* Come on, man, speak up, what is it you want from me, I have to put up my holly. *(pause)* Well to make it short it finally transpired that what he wanted from me was...bread for his brat? Bread? But I have no bread, it doesn't agree with me. Good. Then perhaps a little corn? *(Pause. Normal tone)* That should do it. *(narrative tone)* Corn, yes, I have corn, it's true, in my granaries. But use your head. I give you some corn, a pound, a pound and a half, you bring it back to your child and you make him—if he's still alive—a nice pot of porridge, *(NAGG reacts)* a nice pot and a half of porridge, full of nourishment. Good. The colors come back into his little cheeks—perhaps. And then? *(pause)* I lost patience. *(violently)* Use your head, can't you, use your head, you're on earth, there's no cure for that! *(pause)* It was an exceedingly dry day, I remember, zero by the hygrometer. Ideal weather, for my lumbago. *(Pause. Violently)* But what in God's name do you imagine? That the earth will awake in spring? That the rivers and seas will run with fish again? That there's manna in heaven still for imbeciles like you? *(pause)* Gradually I cooled down, sufficiently at least to ask him how long he had taken on the way. Three whole days. Good. In what condition he had left the child. Deep in sleep. *(forcibly)* But deep in what sleep, deep in what sleep already? *(pause)* Well to make it short I finally offered to take him into my service. He had touched a chord. And then I imagined already that I wasn't much longer for this world. *(He laughs. Pause)* Well? *(pause)* Well? Here if you were careful you might die a nice natural death, in peace and comfort. *(pause)* Well? *(pause)* In the end he asked me would I consent to take in the child as well—if he were still alive. *(pause)* It was the moment I was waiting for. *(pause)* Would I consent to take in the child... *(pause)* I can see him still, down on his knees, his hands flat on the ground, glaring at me with his mad eyes, in defiance of my wishes. *(Pause. Normal tone)* I'll soon have finished with this story. *(pause)* Unless I bring in other characters. *(pause)* But where would I find them? *(pause)* Where would I look for them? *(Pause. He whistles. Enter CLOV)* Let us pray to God.

THE CARETAKER
by Harold Pinter
A house in West London - Aston (20-30)

Here, Aston describes receiving shock treatment in a mental institution.

ASTON: I used to go there quite a bit. Oh, years ago now. But I stopped. I used to like that place. Spent quite a bit of time in there. That was before I went away. Just before. I think that...place had a lot to do with it. They were all...a good bit older than me. But they always used to listen. I thought...they understood what I said. I mean I used to talk to them. I talked too much. That was my mistake. The same in the factory. Standing there, or in the breaks, I used to...talk about things. And these men, they used to listen, whenever I...had anything to say. It was all right. The trouble was, I used to have kind of hallucinations. They weren't hallucinations, they...I used to get the feeling I could see things...very clearly... everything...was so clear...everything used...everything used to get very quiet...everything got very quiet...all this...quiet...and...this clear sight...it was...but maybe I was wrong. Anyway, someone must have said something. I didn't know anything about it. And... some kind of lie must have got around. And this lie went round. I thought people started being funny. In that cafe. The factory. I couldn't understand it. Then one day they took me to a hospital, right outside London. They...got me there. I didn't want to go. Anyway...I tried to get out, quite a few times. But...it wasn't very easy. They asked me questions, in there. Got me in and asked me all sorts of questions. Well, I told them...when they wanted to know ...what my thoughts were. Hmmnn. Then one day...this man... doctor, I suppose...the head one...he was quite a man of... distinction...although I wasn't so sure about that. He called me in. He said...he told me I had something. He said they'd concluded their examination. That's what he said. And he showed me a pile of papers and he said that I'd got something, some complaint. He said...he just said that, you see. You've got...this thing. That's

126

THE CARETAKER

your complaint. And we've decided, he said, that in your interests there's only one course we can take. He said...but I can't...exactly remember...how he put it...he said, we're going to do something to your brain. He said...if we don't, you'll be in here for the rest of your life, but if we do, you stand a chance. You can go out, he said, and live like the others. What do you want to do to my brain, I said to him. But he just repeated what he'd said. Well, I wasn't a fool. I knew I was a minor. I knew he couldn't do anything to me without getting permission. I knew he had to get permission from my mother. So I wrote to ber and told her what they were trying to do. But she signed their form, you see, giving them permission. I know that because he showed me her signature when I brought it up. Well, that night I tried to escape, that night. I spent five hours sawing at one of the bars on the window in this ward. Right throughout the dark. They used to shine a torch over the beds every half hour. So I timed it just right. And then it was nearly done, and a man had a...he had a fit, right next to me. And they caught me, anyway. About a week later they started to come round and do this thing to the brain. We were all supposed to have it done, in this ward. And they came round and did it one at a time. One a night. I was one of the last. And I could see quite clearly what they did to the others. They used to come round with these...I don't know what they were...they looked like big pincers, with wires on, the wires were attached to a little machine. It was electric. They used to hold the man down, and this chief...the chief doctor, used to fit the pincers, something like earphones, he used to fit them on either side of the man's skull. There was a man holding the machine, you see, and he'd...turn it on, and the chief would just press these pincers on either side of the skull and keep them there. Then he'd take them off. They'd cover the man up...and they wouldn't touch him again until later on. Some used to put up a fight, but most of them didn't. They just lay there. Well, they were coming round to me, and the night they came I got up and stood against the wall. They told me to get on the bed, and I knew they had to get me on the bed because if they did it while I was standing

127

THE CARETAKER

up they might break my spine. So I stood up and then one or two of them came for me, well, I was younger then, I was much stronger than I am now, I was quite strong then, I laid one of them out and I had another one round the throat, and then suddenly this chief had these pincers on my skull and I knew he wasn't supposed to do it while I was standing up, that's why I.....anyway, he did it. So I did get out. I got out of the place...but I couldn't walk very well. I don't think my spine was damaged. That was perfectly all right. The trouble was...my thoughts...had become very slow...I couldn't think at all...I couldn't ...get...my thoughts...together...uuuhh...I could...never quite get it ...together. The trouble was, I couldn't hear what people were saying. I couldn't look to the right or the left, I had to look straight in front of me, because if I turned my head round...I couldn't keep ...upright. And I had these headaches. I used to sit in my room. That was when I lived with my mother. And my brother. He was younger than me. And I laid everything out, in order, in my room, all the things I knew were mine, but I didn't die. The thing is, I should have been dead. I should have died. Anyway, I feel much better now. But I don't talk to people now. I steer clear of places like that cafe. I never go into them now. I don't talk to anyone... like that. I've often thought of going back and trying to find the man who did that to me. But I want to do something first. I want to build that shed out in the garden.

THE CARETAKER
by Harold Pinter
A house in West London - Davies (50-60)

Davies has been befriended by Aston, a younger man with brain damage. Sharing a house with Aston, however, becomes more than Davies can bear, as can be seen in the following attack.

DAVIES: What do you expect me to do, stop breathing?
[*(ASTON goes to his bed, and puts on his trousers.)*
ASTON: I'll get a bit of air.]
DAVIES: What do you expect me to do? I tell you, mate, I'm not surprised they took you in. Waking an old man up in the middle of the night, you must be off your nut! Giving me bad dreams, who's responsible, then, for me having bad dreams? If you wouldn't keep mucking me about I wouldn't make no noises! How do you expect me to sleep peaceful when you keep poking me all the time? What do you want me to do, stop breathing?
(He throws the cover off and gets out of bed, wearing his vest, waistcoat and trousers.)
It's getting so freezing in here I have to keep my trousers on to go to bed. I never done that before in my life. But that's what I got to do here. Just because you won't put in any bleeding heating! I've had just about enough with you mucking me about. I've seen better days than you have, man. Nobody ever got me inside one of them places, anyway. I'm a sane man! So don't you start mucking me about. I'll be all right as long as you keep your place. Just you keep your place, that's all. Because I can tell you, your brother's got his eye on you. He knows all about you. I got a friend there, don't you worry about that. I got a true pal there. Treating me like dirt! Why'd you invite me in here in the first place if you was going to treat me like this? You think you're better than me you got another think coming. I know enough. They had you inside one of them places before, they can have you inside again. Your brother's got his eye on you! They can put the pincers on your head again, man! They can have them on again! Any time. All they got to do

is get the word. They'd carry you in there, boy. They'd come here and pick you up and carry you in! They'd keep you fixed! They'd put them pincers on your head, they'd have you fixed! They'd take one look at all this junk I got to sleep with they'd know you were a creamer. That was the greatest mistake they made, you take my tip, letting you get out of that place. Nobody knows what you're at, you go out you come in, nobody knows what you're at! Well, nobody messes me about for long. You think I'm going to do your dirty work? Haaaaahhhhh! You better think again! You want me to do all the dirty work all up and down them stairs just so I can sleep in this lousy filthy hole every night? Not me, boy. Not for you boy. You don't know what you're doing half the time. You're up the creek! You're half off! You can tell it by looking at you. Who ever saw you slip me a few bob? Treating me like a bloody animal! I never been inside a nuthouse!

MONOLOGUES FROM CLASSIC PLAYS

Women's Monologues

PROMETHEUS BOUND
by Aeschylus
translated by J.S. Blackie
A mountain in Scythia - Io (20's)

Io, who has been transformed into a cow by Zeus in order to
save her from the wrath of Hera, tells her unhappy story to
Prometheus.

IO: I will obey,
And in plain speech my chanceful story
    tell;
Though much it grieves me to retrace the
    source,
Whence sprung this god-sent pest, and of
    my shape
Disfigurement abhorred. Night after night
Strange dreams around my maiden pillow
    hovering
Whispered soft temptings. *"O trice-*
    blessed maid,
Why pin'st thou thus in virgin loneliness,
When highest wedlock courts thee?
    Struck by the shaft
Of fond desire for thee Jove burns, and
    pants
To twine his loves with thine. Spurn not,
    O maid,
The proffered bed of Jove; but hie thee
    straight
To Lerne's bosomed mead, where are the
    sheep-folds
And ox-stalls of thy sire, that so the eye
Of Jove, being filled with thee, may cease
    from craving."
Such nightly dreams my restless couch

possessed
Till I, all tears, did force me to unfold
The portent to my father. He to Pytho
Sent frequent messengers, and to Dodona,
Searching the pleasure of the gods; but
   they
With various-woven phrase came back, and
   answers
More doubtful than the quest. At length,
   a clear
And unambiguous voice came to my
   father,
Enjoining, with most strict command, to
   send me
Far from my home, and from my country
   far,
To the extreme bounds of Earth an out-
   cast wanderer,
Else that the fire-faced bolt of Jove should
   smite
Our universal race. By such responses,
Moved of oracular Loxias, my father
Reluctant me reluctant drove from home,
And shut the door against me. What he
   did
He did perforce; Jove's bit was in his
   mouth.
Forthwith my wit was frenzied, and my
   form
Assumed the brute. With maniac bound
   I rushed,
Horned as thou see'st, and with the sharp-
   mouthed sting
Of gad-fly pricked infuriate to the cliff

PROMETHEUS BOUND

Of Lern, and Cenchréa's limpid wave;
While Argus, Earth-born cow-herd, hun-
    dred-eyed,
Followed the winding traces of my path
With sharp observance. Him swift-swoop-
    ing Fate
Snatched unexpected from his sleepless
    guard;
But I from land to land still wander on,
Scourged by the wrath of Heaven's relent-
    less queen.
Thou has my tale; the sequel, if thou
    know'st it,
Is thine to tell; but do not seek, I pray
    thee,
In pity for me, to drop soft lies; for
    nothing
Is worse than the smooth craft of prac-
    tised phrase.

ANTIGONE
by Sophocles
translated by Sir George Young
The royal palace at Thebes - Antigone (18-20)

When Antigone grants her brother a token burial in defiance of the decree of the king, she is sentenced to be buried alive. Here, she welcomes her fate.

ANTIGONE: Thou Grave, my bridal
    chamber! dwelling-place
Hollowed in earth, the everlasting prison
Whither I bend my steps, to join the band
Of kindred, whose more numerous host
    already
Persephone hath counted with the dead;
Of whom I last and far most miserably
Descend, before my term of life is full;
I come, cherishing this hope especially,
To win approval in my father's sight,
Approval too, my mother, in thine, and
    thine
Dear brother! for that with these hands I
    paid
Unto you dead lavement and ordering
And sepulchre-libations; and that now,
Polynices, in the tendance of thy body
I meet with this reward. Yet to the wise
It was no crime, that I did honour thee.
For never had I, even had I been
Mother of children, or if spouse of mine
Lay dead and mouldering, in the state's
    despite
Taken this task upon me. Do you ask
What argument I follow here of law?
One husband dead, another might be mine;

134

ANTIGONE

Sons by another, did I lose the first;
But, sire and mother buried in the grave,
A brother is a branch that grows no more.
Yet I, preferring by this argument
To honour thee in the end, in Creon's
    sight
Appear in that I did so to offend,
And dare to do things heinous, O my
    brother!
And for this cause he hath bid lay hands
    on me,
And leads me, not as wives or brides are
    led,
Unblest with any marriage, any care
Of children; destitute of friends, forlorn,
Yet living, to the chambers of the dead
See me descend. Yet what celestial right
Did I transgress? How should I any more
Look up to heaven, in my adversity?
Whom should I call to aid? Am I not
    come
Through piety to be held impious? If
This is approved in Heaven, why let me
    suffer,
And own that I have sinned; but if the
    sin
Belong to these—O may their punishment
Be measured by the wrongfulness of mine!

Frustrated by Athens' involvement in the Peloponnesian War, Lysistrata convinces the women to withhold all services until peace is achieved. Here, she explains to a commander how governing the states of Greece is no more difficult than unraveling skeins of wool.

LYSISTRATA: When our skein's in a tangle we take it thus
   on our spindles, or haven't you seen us?—
one on this side and one on the other side,
   and we work out the tangles between us.
And that is the way we'll undo this war,
   by exchanging ambassadors, whether
you like it or not, one from either side,
   and we'll work out the tangles together.
[COMMISSIONER: Do you really think that with wools and skeins
   and just being able to spin you
can end these momentous affairs, you fools?]
LYSISTRATA: With any intelligence in you
you statesmen would govern as we work wool,
   and in everything Athens would profit.
[COMMISSIONER: How so? Do tell.]
LYSISTRATA: First, you take raw fleece
   and you wash the beshittedness off it:
just so, you should first lay the city out
   on a washboard and beat out the rotters
and pluck out the sharpers like burrs, and when
   you find tight knots of schemers and plotters
who are out for key offices, card them loose,
   but best tear off their heads in addition.
Then into one basket together card
   all those of a good disposition

LYSISTRATA

be they citizens, resident aliens, friends,
    an ally or an absolute stranger,
even people in debt to the commonwealth,
    you can mix them all in with no danger.
And the cities which Athens has colonized—
    by Zeus, you should try to conceive them
as so many shreddings and tufts of wool
    that are scattered about and not leave them
to lie around loose, but from all of them
    draw the threads in here, and collect them
into one big ball and then weave a coat
    for the people, to warm and protect them.

MEDEA
by Seneca
translated by Frank Justus Miller
The royal palace at Corinth - Medea (20-30)

Medea has sacrificed all for Jason, and when he rejects her and
plans to marry another woman, she sinks into a dark despair and
begins to plan revenge.

MEDEA: Ye gods of wedlock, thou the
    nuptial couch's guard,
Lucina, thou from whom that tamer of the
    deep,
The Argo's pilot, learned to guide his
    pristine bark,
And Neptune, thou stern ruler of the
    ocean's depths,
And Titan, by whose rays the shining day
    is born,
Thou triformed maiden Hecate, whose con-
    scious beams
With splendor shine upon the mystic wor-
    shipers—
Upon ye all I call, the powers of heaven,
    the gods
Whose aid Medea may more boldly claim,
    thou world
Of endless night, th' antipodes of heavenly
    realms,
Ye damned ghosts, thou lord of hades'
    dark domain,
Whose mistress was with trustier pledge
    won to thy side—
Before ye all this baleful prayer I bring:
    Be near!
Be near! Ye crime-avenging furies, come

and loose
Your horrid locks with serpent coils en-
twined, and grasp
With bloody hands the smoking torch; be
near as once
Ye stood in dread array beside my wedding
couch.
Upon this new-made bride destruction
send, and death
Upon the king and all the royal line!
But he,
My husband, may he live to meet some
heavier doom;
This curse I imprecate upon his head;
may he, .
Through distant lands, in want, in exile
wander, scorned
And houseless. Nay, may he once more
my favor woo;
A stranger's threshold may he seek where
now he walks
A well-known guest; and—this the black-
est curse I know—
May children rise to him to emulate their
sire,
Their mother's image bear.—Now won is
vengeance, won!
For I have children borne.—Nay, nay, 'tis
empty plaints
And useless words I frame. Shall I not
rather rush
Against the foe and dash the torches from
their hands,
The light from heaven? Does Father

Phoebus suffer this?
Do men behold his face, as, seated in his
car,
He rolls along th' accustomed track of
sky serene?
Why does he not return to morning's
gates, the law
Of heaven reversing? Grant that I be
borne aloft
In my ancestral car! Give me the reins,
O sire,
Thy fiery team grant me to guide with
lines of flame.
Then Corinth, though with double shore
delaying fate,
Herself consumed with fire, shall light
two seas with flame.
But no, this course alone remains, that
I myself
Should bear the wedding torch, with ac-
quiescent prayers,
And slay the victims on the altars con-
secrate.
Thyself inspect the entrails, and seek there
the way
By prayer, if still, O soul, thou livest, if
there still
Remaineth aught of old-time strength in
thee! Away
With woman's fears! Put on thy heart
a beast-plate hard
And chill as Caucasus! Then all the
wizard arts
That Phasis knew, or Pontus, shall be

seen again
In Corinth. Now with mad, unheard of,
  dreadful deeds,
Whereat high heaven and earth below
  shall pale and quake,
My pregnant soul is teeming; and my
  heart is full
Of pictured wounds and death and slaugh-
  ter.—Ah, too long
On trifling ills I dwell. These were my
  virgin deeds.
Now that a mother's pains I've felt, my
  larger heart
Must larger crimes conceive. Then pas-
  sion, gird thyself,
Put on thy strength, and for the issue
  now prepare!
Let my rejection pay as dread a fee as
  when,
Of old, through impious deeds of blood,
  I came to him.
Come, break through slow delay, and let
  the home once won
By crime, by equal deeds of crime be done
  away!

MEDEA
by Seneca
translated by Frank Justus Miller
The royal palace at Corinth - Medea (20-30)

Close to madness, Medea reviews the crimes she has committed
for Jason, including the grisly death of her own brother.

MEDEA: We are undone! How harsh
   upon mine ears doth grate
The song! and even now I cannot com-
   prehend
The vast extent of woe that hath befallen
   me.
Could Jason prove so false? Bereft of
   native land,
And home, and kingdom, could he leave
   me here alone
On foreign shores? Oh, cruel, could he
   quite reject
My sum of service, he who saw the fire
   and sea
With crime o'ercome for his dear sake?
   And does he think
That thus the fatal chapter can be ended?
   Wild,
Devoid of reason, sick of soul, my swift
   mind darts
In all directions seeking whence revenge
   may come!
I would he had a brother! But his
   wife—'gainst her
Be aimed the blow! Can thus my wrongs
   be satisfied?
Nay, nay—to meet my sum of woe must
   be heaped high

142

MEDEA

The crimes of Greece, of strange barbaric
  lands, and those
Which even thy hands have not known.
  Now lash thy soul
With memory's scourge, and call thy dark
  deeds in review:
The glory of thy father's kingdom reft
  away;
Thy brother, guiltless comrade of thy
  guilty flight,
All hewn in pieces and his corpse strewn
  on the deep,
To break his royal father's heart; and,
  last of crimes,
Old Pelias by his daughters slain at thy
  command.
O impious one, what streams of blood
  have flowed to work
Thy ends! And yet, not one of all my
  crimes by wrath
Was prompted. Love, ill-omened love,
  suggested all.
Yet, what could Jason else have done,
  compelled to serve
Another's will, another's law? He should
  have died
Before he yielded to the tyrant's will.
  Nay, nay,
Thou raging passion, speak not so! For,
  if he may,
I would that Jason still may live and
  still be mine,
As once he was; if not, yet may he still
  live on,

143

And, mindful of my merits, live without
   my aid.
The guilt is Creon's all, who with un-
   bridled power
Dissolves the marriage bond, my children
   separates
From me who bore them, yea, and makes
   the strongest pledge,
Though ratified with straightest oath, of
   none effect.
Let him alone sustain my wrath; let
   Creon pay
The debt of guilt he owes! His palace
   will I bring
To utter desolation; and the whirling fire
To far-off Malea's crags shall send its
   lurid glare.

TAMBURLAINE THE GREAT
by Christopher Marlowe
Medieval Persia - Zenocrate (20-30)

Following her ruthless husband's bloody conquest of Damascus,
Zenocrate grieves for the dead.

ZENOCRATE: Wretched Zenocrate! that liv'st to see
Damascus' walls dy'd with Egyptian blood,
Thy father's subjects and thy countrymen;
Thy streets strow'd with dissevered joints of men
And wounded bodies gasping yet for life:
But most accurst, to see the sun-bright troop
Of heavenly virgins and unspotted maids
(Whose looks might make the angry god of arms
To break his sword and mildly treat of love)
On horsemen's lances to be hoisted up
And guiltlessly endure a cruel death:
For every fell and stout Tartarian steed,
That stamp'd on others with their thundering hoofs,
When all their riders charg'd their quivering spears,
Began to check the ground and rein themselves,
Gazing upon the beauty of their looks.
Ah Tamburlaine! wert thou the cause of this,
That term'st Zenocrate thy dearest love?
Whose lives were dearer to Zenocrate
Than her own life, or aught save thine own love.
But see another bloody spectacle!
Ah, wretched eyes, the enemies of my heart,
How are ye glutted with these grievous objects,
And tell my soul more tales of bleeding ruth!
See, see, Anippe, if they breathe or no.
[ANIPPE: No breath, nor sense, nor motion in them both.
Ah, madam! this their slavery hath enforc'd,
And ruthless cruelty of Tamburlaine.]
ZENOCRATE: Earth, cast up fountains from thy entrails,

TAMBURLAINE THE GREAT

And wet thy cheeks for their untimely deaths!
Shake with their weight in sign of fear and grief!
Blush, Heaven, that gave them honour at their birth
And let them die a death so barbarous!
Those that are proud of fickle empery
And place their chiefest good in earthly pomp,
Behold the Turk and his great Emperess!
Thou, that in conduct of thy happy stars
Sleep'st every night with conquest on thy brows,
And yet would'st shun the wavering turns of war,
In fear and feeling of the like distress
Behold the Turk and his great Emperess!
Ah, mighty Jove and holy Mohomet,
Pardon my love!—O, pardon his contempt
Of earthly fortune and respect of pity,
And let not conquest, ruthlessly pursu'd,
Be equally against his life incens'd
In this great Turk and hapless Emperess!
And pardon me that was not mov'd with ruth
To see them live so long in misery!
Ah, what may chance to thee, Zenocrate?

THE TAMING OF THE SHREW
by William Shakespeare
Medieval Padua - Kate (20-30)

The tamed shrew here counsels women on the proper way to
manage a married relationship.

KATE: Fie, fie, unknit that threatening unkind brow
And dart not scornful glances from those eyes
To wound thy lord, thy king, thy governor.
It blots thy beauty as frosts do bite the meads,
Confounds thy fame as whirlwinds shake fair
    buds,
And in no sense is meet or amiable.
A woman moved is like a foundation troubled,
Muddy, ill-seeming, thick, bereft of beauty,
And while it is so, none so dry or thirsty
Will deign to sip or touch one drop of it.
Thy husband is thy lord, thy life, thy keeper,
Thy head, thy sovereign—one that cares for thee,
And for thy maintenance commits his body
To painful labor both by sea and land,
To watch the night in storms, the day in cold,
Whilst thou li'st warm at home, secure and safe;
And craves no other tribute at thy hands
But love, fair looks, and true obedience:
Too little payment for so great a debt.
Such duty as the subject owes the prince,
Even such a woman oweth to her husband,
And when she is froward, peevish, sullen, sour,
And not obedient to his honest will,
What is she but a foul contending rebel
And graceless traitor to her loving lord?
I am ashamed that women are so simple
To offer war where they should kneel for peace,
Or seek for rule, supremacy, and sway,

THE TAMING OF THE SHREW

When they are bound to serve, love, and obey.
Why are our bodies soft and weak and smooth,
Unapt to toil and trouble in the world,
But that our soft conditions and our hearts
Should well agree with our external parts?
Come, come, you froward and unable worms,
My mind hath been as big as one of yours,
My heart as great, my reason haply more,
To bandy word for word and frown for frown.
But now I see our lances are but straws,
Our strength as weak, our weakness past compare,
That seeming to be most which we indeed least are.
Then vail your stomachs, for it is no boot,
And place your hands below your husband's foot,
In token of which duty, if he please,
My hand is ready, may it do him ease.

A MIDSUMMER NIGHT'S DREAM
by William Shakespeare
An enchanted forest - Titania (30-40)

When Oberon feels that Titania has betrayed him, he confronts her with his jealous suspicions. The willful queen offers the following response.

TITANIA: These are the forgeries of jealousy:
And never, since the middle summer's spring,
Met we on hill, in dale, forest, or mead,
By pave'd fountain or by rushy brook,
Or in the beache'd margent of the sea,
To dance our ringlets to the whistling wind,
But with thy brawls thou hast disturbed our sport.
Therefore the winds, piping to us in vain,
As in revenge, have sucked up from the sea
Contagious fogs; which, falling in the land,
Hath every pelting river made so proud,
That they have overborne their continents.
The ox hath therefore stretched his yoke in vain,
The plowman lost his sweat, and the green corn
Hath rotted ere his youth attained a beard;
The fold stands empty in the drowne'd field,
And crows are fatted with murrion flock,
The nine men's morris is filled up with mud;
And the quaint mazes in the wonton green,
For lack of tread, are undistinguishable.
The human mortals want their winter here;
No night is now with hymn or carol blest.
Therefore the moon, the governess of floods,
Pale in her anger, washes all the air,
That rheumatic diseases do abound.
And thorough this distemperature we see
The seasons alter: hoary-headed frosts
Fall in the fresh lap of the crimson rose,

A MIDSUMMER NIGHT'S DREAM

And on old Hiems' thin and icy crown
An odorous chaplet of sweet summer buds
Is, as in mockery, set. The spring, the summer,
The childing autumn, angry winter, change
Their wonted liveries; and the maze'd world,
By their increase, now knows not which is which.
And this same progeny of evils comes
From our debate, from our dissension;
We are their parents and original.
[OBERON: Do you amend it, then; it lies in you:
Why should Titania cross her Oberon?
I do but beg a little changeling boy,
To be my henchman.]
TITANIA: Set your heart to rest.
The fairy land buys not the child of me.
His mother was a vot'ress of my order,
And, in the spice'd Indian air, by night,
Full often hath she gossiped by my side,
And sat with me on Neptune's yellow sands,
Marking th' embarkèd traders on the flood;
When we have laughed to see the sails conceive
And grow big-bellied with the wanton wind;
Which she, with pretty and with swimming gait
Following—her womb then rich with my young
    squire—
Would imitate, and sail upon the land,
To fetch me trifles, and return again,
As from a voyage, rich with merchandise.
But she, being mortal, of that boy did die;
And for her sake do I rear up her boy,
And for her sake I will not part with him.

THE MALCONTENT
by John Marston
The Duke's court in Genoa - Aurelia (20-30)

Having fallen victim to the vicious intrigues of the court, the
Duchess finds herself facing exile.

AURELIA: It is too good: blessed spirit of my lord,
O, in what orb so e'er thy soul is thron'd,
Behold me worthily most miserable:
O let the anguish of my contrite spirit
Entreat some reconciliation:
If not, O joy, triumph in my just grief,
Death is the end of woes, and tears' relief.
[PIETRO: Belike your lord not lov'd you, was unkind.]
AURELIA: O heaven!
As the soul lov'd the body, so lov'd he,
'Twas death to him to part my presence, heaven
To see me pleased:
Yet I, like a wretch given o'er to hell,
Brake all the sacred rites of marriage,
To clip a base ungentle faithless villain:
O God, a very pagan reprobate—
What should I say?—ungrateful throws me out,
For whom I lost soul, body, fame, and honour:
But 'tis most fit: why should a better fate
Attend on any, who forsake chaste sheets,
Fly the embrace of a devoted heart,
Join'd by a solemn vow 'fore God and man,
To taste the brackish blood of beastly lust,
In an adulterous touch? Oh ravenous immodesty,
Insatiate impudence of appetite!
Look, here's your end, for mark what sap in dust,
What sin in good, even so much love in lust:
Joy to thy ghost, sweet Lord, pardon to me.

THE MAID'S TRAGEDY
by Francis Beaumont and John Fletcher
The city of Rhodes - Aspatia (20's)

When the king decrees that Aspatia may not marry Amintor, the
young woman takes comfort in the company of her ladies-in-
waiting and here counsels them on how best to fall in love.

ASPATIA: Away, you are not sad; force
  it no further.
Good Gods, how well you look! Such a
  full colour
Young bashful brides put on. Sure, you
  are new married!
[ANTIPHILA: Yes, madam, to your grief.]
ASPATIA: Alas, poor wenches!
Go learn to love first; learn to lose yourselves;
Learn to be flatter'd, and believe, and bless
The double tongue that did it. Make a
  faith
Out of the miracles of ancient lovers,
Such as speak truth, and died in't; and,
  like me,
Believe all faithful, and be miserable.
Did you ne'er love yet, wenches? Speak,
  Olympias;
Thou hast an easy temper, fit for stamp.
[OLYMPIAS: Never.]
ASPATIA: Nor you, Antiphila?
[ANTIPHILA: Nor I.]
ASPATIA: Then, my good girls, be more
  than women, wise:
At least be more than I was; and be
  sure
You credit anything the light gives light
  to,

152

THE MAID'S TRAGEDY

Before a man. Rather believe the sea
Weeps for the ruin'd merchant, when he
  roars;
Rather, the wind courts but the pregnant
  sails,
When the strong cordage cracks; rather,
  the sun
Comes but to kiss the fruit in wealthy
  autumn,
When all falls blasted. If you needs must
  love,
(Forced by ill fate) take to your maiden
  bosoms
Two dead-cold aspicks, and of them make
  lovers:
They cannot flatter, nor forswear; one kiss
Makes a long peace for all. But man,
Oh, that beast man! Come, let's be sad
  my girls!
That down-cast of thine eye, Olympias,
Shows a fine sorrow. Mark, Antiphila;
Just such another was the nymph Œnone,
When Paris brought home Helen. Now, a
  tear;
And then thou art a piece expressing fully
The Carthage queen, when, from a cold
  sea-rock,
Full with her sorrow, she tied fast her
  eyes
To the fair Trojan ships; and, having lost
  them,
Just as thine eyes do, down stole a tear.
  Antiphila,
What would this wench do, if she were

   Aspatia?

Here she would stand, till some more
   pitying god

Turn'd her to marble ! 'Tis enough, my
   wench!

Show me the piece of needlework you
   wrought.

THE ATHEIST'S TRAGEDY
by Cyril Tourneur
A 16th century baronial estate - Castabella (20-30)

When the evil D'Amville attempts to seduce virtuous Castabella, she denounces his adulterous lust to God.

CASTABELLA: O God! is thy unlimited
And infinite omnipotence less free
Because thou dost no ill? Or if
You argue merely out of Nature, do
You not degenerate from that, and are
You not unworthy the prerogative
Of Nature's masterpiece, when basely you
Prescribe your self authority and law
From their examples whom you should command?
I could confute you; but the horror of
The argument confounds my understanding.—
Sir, I know
You do but try me in your son's behalf;
Suspecting that my strength and youth of blood
Cannot contain themselves with impotence.—
Believe me (sir)
I never wrong'd him. If it be your lust,
O quench it on their prostituted flesh,
Whose trade of sin can please desire with more
Delight, and less offence.—
The poison of your breath,
Evaporated from so foul a soul,
Infects the air more than the damps that rise
From bodies but half rotten in their graves.
[D'AMVILLE: Kiss me. I warrant thee my breath is sweet.
These dead men's bones lie here of purpose to
Invite us to supply the number of
The living. Come; we'll get young bones and do't.
I will enjoy thee. No? Nay then invoke

Your great suppos'd protector; I will do't.]
CASTABELLA: Suppos'd protector? Are y' an atheist? Then,
I know my prayers and tears are spent in vain.
O patient Heav'n! Why dost thou not express
Thy wrath in thunderbolts, to tear the frame
Of man in pieces? How can earth endure
The burden of this wickedness without
An earthquake? Or the angry face of Heav'n
Be not enflam'd with lightning?
[D'AMVILLE: Conjure up
The Devil and his dam; cry to the graves;
The dead can hear thee; invocate their help.]
CASTABELLA: O would this grave might open, and my body
Were bound to the dead carcass of a man
For ever, ere it entertain the lust
Of this detested villain.

THE CONSTANT PRINCE
by Pedro Calderon de la Barca
translated by Denis Florence MacCarthy
The court of the King of Fez, Morocco - Phenix (20's)

The young princess has discovered that her father intends to
marry her to a man she does not love, and as a result she can no
longer be moved by the earth's beauty.

PHENIX: Ah! no more can gladden me
Sunny shores, or dark projections,
Where in emulous reflections
Blend the rival land and sea;
When, alike in charms and powers
Where the woods and waves are meeting—
Flowers with foam are seen competing—
Sparkling foam with snow-white flowers;
For the garden, envious grown
Of the curling waves of ocean,
Loves to imitate their motion;
And the amorous zephyr, blown
Out to sea from fragrant bowers,
In the shining waters laving
Back returns, and makes the waving
Leaves an ocean of bright flowers:
When the sea too, sad to view
Its barren waste of waves forlorn,
Striveth swiftly to adorn
All its realm, and to subdue
The pride of its majestic mien,
To second laws it doth subject
Its nature, and with sweet effect
Blends fields of blue with waves of green.
Coloured now like heaven's blue dome,
Now plumed as if from verdant bowers,
The garden seems a sea of flowers,

THE CONSTANT PRINCE

The sea a garden of bright foam:
How deep my pain must be, is plain,
Since naught delights my heart or eye,
Nor earth, nor air, nor sea, nor sky.

THE KING, THE GREATEST ALCALDE
by Lope Felix de Vega Carpio
translated by John Garrett Underhill
Leon, Spain - Elvira (20-30)

Elvira has been raped by the evil Don Tello. Here, she tells her
story to the king and begs for justice.

ELVIRA: The moment my sorrows
To thee might complain,
Castilian Alfonso
Who governs all Spain,
I broke from my prison,
The cell which confined,
To petition thy justice,
Royal mercy to find.
Daughter to Nuño
Of Aibar am I,
In honor and station
Well-known and high
Through all these lands.
Sancho of Roelas
Sought me in love;
My father consenting
His suit did approve.
Don Tello of Neira
By Sancho was served,
Who begged his lord's license
Ere the rite be observed.
He came with his sister,
Our sponsors they stood.
He saw me, he craved me
And foul plot he brewed.
He put off the wedding,
He came to my door
With men bearing weapons

THE KING, THE GREATEST ALCALDE

And black masks before.
I was borne to his dwelling,
With treacherous art
He sought to destroy me,
My chaste firmness of heart.
And then from that dwelling
I was haled to a wood,
A farm house adjacent,
A fourth league removed.
There, where only
Was tangle of trees,
Which the sun could not peep through
To be witness with these—
The trees heard may mourning,
My sad, long lament.
My locks tell the story—
What struggles I bent
Against his offending,
And all the flowers know
How I left on their blooming
Fond tresses of woe;
My eyes tell the story—
What tears there I shed
That the hard rock might soften
Like down to the head.
I shall live now in weeping,
How shall she retain
Contentment or pleasure
Whose honor lies slain?
Yet in this I am happy—
That here I complain
To the Greatest Alcalde
That governs in Spain.
I plead for his justice,

THE KING, THE GREATEST ALCALDE

I beg of his rule
Pity for wronging
So false and so cruel.
This be my petition,
Alfonso, whose feet
My poor lips with kisses
Humbly entreat.
And so may the offspring
Rule conquered and free
The parts of thy kingdom
The Moor holds in fee,
Through happy war. Poor
My tongue in praise,
But endless song and story
Shall prolong thy days!

THE CID
by Pierre Corneille
translated by Florence Kendrick Cooper
Seville - Chimène (20's)

The daughter of the Count of Gormaz here confronts her father's
murderer, the Cid, who also happens to be the man she loves.

CHIMÈNE: Ah ! Roderick, strangely
  does my changeful heart
Defend thee who hast saved thy father's
  fame.
If my distracted mind has cruel seemed,
'T is not with blame for thee, but in despair.
The ardor of a high, unbroken spirit
That cannot brook an insult, well I know.
It was thy duty taught thee, but, alas!
In doing thine, thou teachest me mine
  own.
The very terror of thy deed compels;
For, as thy father's name thou hast restored
Mine also calls upon his child for vengeance.
But, oh! my love for thee drives me to
  madness!
My father's loss by other hand had left
The solace of thy presence and thy love,
A consolation sweet in misery.
I still had felt in grief thy sympathy,
And loved the hand that wiped my tears
  away.
But now, in losing him thee too I lose;
This victory o'er my love his fame demands,
And duty, with the face of an assassin,
Drives me to work thy ruin and mine own.
For in my heart no more than in thine
  own

162

THE CID

Must courage yield to luring dreams of
    love.
My strength must equal thine. In thine
    offense
Thou hast but proved thy worth. By
    thine own death
Alone can I be worthy of thy love.

THE CHANGELING
by Thomas Middleton and William Rowley
A seaport on the east coast of Spain - Beatrice (20-30)

Beatrice persuades her servant, Deflores, to murder her fiance
so that she can marry the man she loves. In return, however,
Deflores demands that she sleep with him. On the eve of her
wedding, Beatrice fears that her husband will detect her non-
virginal status on their wedding night.

BEATRICE: This fellow has undone me endlessly,
Never was bride so fearfully distrest;
The more I think upon th'ensuing night,
And whom I am to cope with in embraces,
One both ennobled both in blood and mind,
So clear in understanding (that's my plague now),
Before whose judgment will my fault appear
Like malefactors' crimes before tribunals:
There is no hiding on't, the more I dive
Into my own distress; how a wise man
Stands for a great calamity. There's no venturing
Into his bed, what course soe'er I light upon,
Without my shame, which may grow up to danger;
He cannot but in justice strangle me
As I lie by him, as a cheater use me;
'Tis a precious craft to play with a false die
Before a cunning gamester. Here's his closet
The key left in't, and he abroad i'th'park;
Sure 'twas forgot, I'll be so bold as look in't.
Bless me! A right physician's closet 'tis,
Set round with vials, every one her mark too.
Sure he does practise physic for his own use,
Which may be safely call'd your great man's wisdom.
What manuscript lies here? The Book of Experiment,
Call'd *Secrets in Nature:* so 'tis, 'tis so.
'How to know whether a woman be with child or no.'

THE CHANGELING

I hope I am not yet; if he should try though!
Let me see, folio 45. Here 'tis;
The leaf tuckt down upon't, the place suspicious.
'If you would know
Whether a woman be with child, or not,
    give her two spoonfuls of the white water in Glass C.'—
Where's that Glass C? O yonder, I see't now,—
'And if she be with child,
She sleeps full twelve hours after, if not, not.'
None of that water comes into my belly.
I'll know you from a hundred, I could break
You now or turn you into milk, and so
Beguile the master of the mystery,
But I'll look to you. Ha! that which is next,
Is ten times worse. 'How to know whether
A woman be a maid, or not'; if that
Should be apply'd, what would become of me?
Belike he has a strong faith of my purity,
That never yet made proof; but this he calls
'A merry sleight, but true experiment,
    the author Antonius Mizaldus. Give the party you suspect the
    quantity of a spoonful of the water in the glass M, which upon her
    that is a maid, makes three several effects: 'twill make her
    incontinently gape, then fall into a sudden sneezing, last into a
    violent laughing, else dull, heavy and lumpish.'
Where had I been?
I fear it, yet 'tis seven hours to bed time.

165

WOMEN BEWARE WOMEN
by Thomas Middleton
Florence - Isabella (20-30)

When her aunt's marriage is announced, Isabella ruminates on the place of women and their responsibility to accept the husbands chosen for them.

ISABELLA: *(Aside)* Marry a fool!
Can there be greater misery to a woman
That means to keep her days true to her husband,
And know no other man! So virtue wills it.
Why; how can I obey and honour him,
But I must needs commit idolatry?
A fool is but the image of a man,
And that but ill-made neither: oh the heart-breakings
Of miserable maids, where love's enforc'd!
The best condition is but bad enough;
When women have their choices, commonly
They do but buy their thraldoms, and bring great portions
To men to keep 'em in subjection,
As if a fearful prisoner should bribe
The keeper to be good to him, yet lies in still,
And glad of a good usage, a good look sometimes.
By'r Lady, no misery surmounts a woman's.
Men buy their slaves, but women buy their masters;
Yet honesty and love makes all this happy,
And next to angels', the most blest estate.
That Providence, that has made ev'ry poison
Good for some use, and sets four warring elements
At peace in man, can make a harmony
In things that are most strange to human reason.
Oh but this marriage!—What, are you sad too, Uncle?
Faith, then there's a whole household down together:
Where shall I go to seek my comfort now
When my best friend's distress'd? what is't afflicts you, sir?

WOMEN BEWARE WOMEN
by Thomas Middleton
Florence - Bianca (20-30)

When Bianca's beauty captures the interest of the Duke, she allows him to seduce her.   Here, she laments betraying her husband.

BIANCA: *(Aside)* Now bless me from a blasting; I saw that now
Fearful for any woman's eye to look on;
Infectious mists and mildews hang at's eyes:
The weather of a doomsday dwells upon him.
Yet since mine honour's leprous, why should I
Preserve that fair that caus'd the leprosy?
Come poison all at once.—*(To GUARDIANO)*   Thou in whose
baseness. The bane of virtue broods, I'm bound in soul
Eternally to curse thy smooth-brow'd treachery,
That wore the fair veil of a friendly welcome,
And I a stranger; think upon't, 'tis worth it.
Murders pil'd up upon a guilty spirit
At his last breath will not lie heavier
Than this betraying act upon thy conscience:
Beware of off'ring the first-fruits to sin;
His weight is deadly who commits with strumpets,
After they have been abas'd, and made for use;
If they offend to th'death, as wise men know,
How much more they then that first make 'em so!
I give thee that to feed on; I'm made bold now,
I thank thy treachery; sin and I'm acquainted,
No couple greater; and I'm like that great one,
Who, making politic use of a base villain,
He likes the treason well, but hates the traitor;
So hate I thee, slave.

TWO PRECIOUS MAIDENS RIDICULED
by Molìere
translated by Albert Bermel
The house of Gorgibus, Paris - 17th Century - Magdelon (18-20)

Here Magdelon, a self-centered and rather silly young woman, explains the rules of courtship and chivalry to her father.

MAGDELON: Good Gothic, if everybody thought that, a novel would end as soon as it started. What if Cyrus married Mandane in Chapter One or Aronce were wedded to Clélie without any obstacles instead of having to wait until the end of Volume Ten?
[GORGIBUS: What has all this to-do got to do with me?]
MAGDELON: Cousin Cathos will tell you the same thing, Father; marriage can take place only after all the other adventures. To make himself acceptable, a lover must know how to utter beautiful thoughts, to pour out tenderness, sweetness, and passion, and—very important—his wooing must follow the rules. First, he meets the maiden he loves in church or out walking or at a public ceremony; or he must be led by Fate—in other words, a friend or relative—to her home, from which he emerges in a dream or state of melancholy. For a time he hides his devotion from his beloved, but he does pay her several visits and joins in discussions of gallantry; this never fails to edify the assembled guests. The day comes for his declaration and this is usually made along some garden path, when the rest of the company has moved out of range. The message of love promptly enrages us—our blushes indicate this clearly—and the young man is thereby banished from our presence, for a short time. He next finds some way of appeasing us; gradually we soften to his passionate recital, and he draws out our own vows, which are unbearably painful to confess. After that come the adventures: the rivals who throw themselves in the way of true love; the persecutions of the fathers; the jealousy caused by misunderstanding; the accusations, the heartaches, the abductions, and other assorted complications. That's how these affairs unwind; there are rules of chivalry and breeding that must be observed. But to leap from one

end of the love affair to the other, to substitute a marriage contract for an amour, to seize the novel by its tail—nothing, Father, nothing could be more commercial, and the mere thought of it makes my heart shiver.

BERENICE
by Jean Racine
translated by R.B. Boswell
The imperial palace in Rome - Berenice (20-30)

The Queen of Palestine has been brought to Rome to marry
Titus, the Emperor. When a friend warns that marriage to
foreigners isn't well regarded, Berenice points out the absolute
authority of the Emperor.

BERENICE: The time is gone when I
  could tremble.
The Emperor loves me, and his word
  has pow'r
Unlimited. He'll see the senate bring me
Their homage, and the people crown his
  statues
With garlands.
Have you seen this
  night's rare splendour?
Are not your eyes fill'd with its dazzling
  glory?
That funeral pyre, the darkness lost in
  light
Of blazing torches, armies with their
  eagles,
Long lines of lictors, consuls, senators,
A crowd of Kings, and all with glory
  borrow'd
From Titus; gold and purple which enhanced
His majesty, and bays that crown'd the
  victor;
All eyes of visitors from every land
Turning their eager gaze on him alone;
That noble carriage, and that air benign,—
Good gods! with what affection and respect

170

BERENICE

All hearts assured him of their loyalty!
Could any then behold him and not think,
As I did, that, however lowly born,
The world would still have own'd him as
    its master?
But whither does my fond remembrance
    wander?
All Rome, Phoenice, at this very moment
Offers her vows for Titus, and with smoke
Of sacrifice inaugurates his reign.
Why should we linger? Let us add our
    pray'rs
For his success to Heav'n that watches
    o'er him.
Then straightway, without waiting to be
    summon'd,
I'll seek him, and in loving colloquy
Say all that warm affection, long repress'd,
Inspires in hearts contented with each
    other.

PHAEDRA
by Racine
translated by Robert Lowell
Ancient Greece - Phaedra (20-30)

Here, Phaedra confesses her forbidden passion for Hippolytus,
her stepson, to her old nurse.

PHAEDRA: My evil comes from farther off. In May,
in brilliant Athens, on my marriage day,
I turned aside for shelter from the smile
of Theseus. Death was frowning in an aisle—
Hippolytus! I saw his face, turned white!
My lost and dazzled eyes saw only night,
capricious burnings flickered through my bleak
abandoned flesh. I could not breathe or speak.
I faced my flaming executioner,
Aphrodite, my mother's murderer!
I tried to calm her wrath by flowers and praise,
I built her a temple, fretted months and days
on decoration. I even hoped to find
symbols and stays for my distracted mind,
searching the guts of sacrificial steers.
Yet when my erring passions, mutineers
to virtue, offered incense at the shrine
of love, I failed to silence the malign
Goddess. Alas, my hungry open mouth,
thirsting with adoration, tasted drouth—
Venus resigned her altar to my new lord—
and even while I was praying, I adored
Hippolytus above the sacred flame,
now offered to his name I could not name.
I fled him, yet he stormed me in disguise,
and seemed to watch me with his father's eyes.
I even turned against myself, screwed up
my slack courage to fury, and would not stop

172

PHAEDRA

shrieking and raging, till half-dead with love
and the hatred of a stepmother, I drove
Hippolytus in exile from the rest
and strenuous wardship of his father's breast.
Then I could breathe, Oenone; he was gone;
my lazy, nerveless days meandered on
through dreams and daydreams, like a stately carriage
touring the level landscape of my marriage.
Yet nothing worked. My husband sent me here
to Troezen, far from Athens; once again the dear
face shattered me; I saw Hippolytus
each day, and felt my ancient, venomous
passion tear my body limb from limb;
naked, Venus was clawing down her victim.
What could I do? Each moment, terrified
by loose diseased emotions, now I cried
for death to save my glory and expel
my gloomy frenzy from this world, my hell.
And yet your tears and words bewildered me,
and so endangered my tranquillity,
at last I spoke. Nurse, I shall not repent,
if you will leave me the passive content
of dry silence and solitude.

THE PROVOK'D WIFE
by Sir John Vanbrugh
17th century England - Mistress Bracegirdle (30-40)

Here, an actress speaks to the audience in a prologue in which she condemns the playwright for having the audacity to have written three plays at once.

MISTRESS BRACEGIRDLE:
Since 'tis the intent and business of the stage,
To copy out the follies of the age;
To hold to every man a faithful glass,
And shew him of what species he's an ass:
I hope the next that teaches in the school,
Will shew our author he's a scribling fool.
And that the satyr may be sure to bite,
Kind Heav'n, inspire some venom'd priest to write,
And grant some ugly lady may indite!
For I wou'd have him lash'd, by heavens! I wou'd,
Till his presumption swam away in blood.
Three plays at once proclaim a face of brass—
No matter what they are; that's not the case—
To write three plays, ev'n that's to be an ass.
But what I least forgive—he knows it too,
For to his cost he lately has known you.
Experience shews, to many a writers smart,
You hold a court where mercy ne're had part;
So much of the old serpent's sting you have,
You love to damn, as Heav'n delights to save.
In foreign parts, let a bold voluntiere
For publick good, upon the stage appear,
He meets ten thousand smiles to dissipate his fear.
All tickle on th' adventuring young beginner,
And only scourge th' incorragible sinner;
They touch indeed his faults, but with a hand
So gentle, that his merit still may stand:

THE PROVOK'D WIFE

Kindly they buoy the follies of his pen,
That he may shun 'em when he writes again.
But 'tis not so in this good-natur'd town;
All's one, an ox, a poet, or a crown:
Old England's play was always knocking down.

THE PROVOK'D WIFE
by Sir John Vanbrugh
17th century England - Lady Brute (30's)

Having been rudely chastised for her questionable morality by her bitter husband, Lady Brute fumes as she considers the possibilities for her revenge.

LADY BRUTE: The devil's in the fellow, I think!—I was told before I married him, that thus 'twou'd be: but I thought I had charms enough to govern him; and that where there was an estate, a woman must needs be happy; so my vanity has deceiv'd me, and my ambition has made me uneasie. But some comfort still! If one wou'd be reveng'd of him, these are good times; a woman may have a gallant, and a separate maintenance too.—The surly puppy!—Yet he's a fool for't, for hitherto he has been no monster: but who knows how far he may provoke me? I never lov'd him, yet I have been ever true to him; and that, in spight of all the attacks of art and nature upon a poor weak womans heart, in favour of a tempting lover. Methinks so noble a defence as I have made, shou'd be rewarded with a better usage.—Or who can tell?—Perhaps a good part of what I suffer from my husband, may be a judgement upon me for my cruelty to my lover.—Lord, with what pleasure cou'd I indulge that thought, were there but a possibility of finding arguments to make it good!—And how do I know but there may?— Let me see.—What opposes?—My matrimonial vow?—Why, what did I vow? I think I promis'd to be true to my husband. Well; and he promis'd to be kind to me. But he han't kept his word.—Why then I'm absolv'd from mine.—Ay, that seems clear to me. The argument's good between the king and the people; why not between the husband and the wife? O, but that condition was not exprest.— No matter, 'twas understood. Well, by all I see, if I argue the matter a little longer with my self, I shan't find so many bugbears in the way as I thought I shou'd. Lord, what fine notions of virtue do we women take up upon the credit of old foolish philosophers! Virtue it's own reward, virtue's this, virtue's that;—virtue's an ass, and a gallant's worth forty on't.

176

THE BEAUX-STRATAGEM
by George Farquhar
Lichfield, England - Early 18th century - Mrs. Sullen (40-50)

Here, Mrs. Sullen offers jaded counsel to young Dorinda, who
fancies herself in love.

MRS. SULLEN: Country pleasures! racks and torments! Dost
think, child, that my limbs were made for leaping of ditches, and
clambering over stiles? or that my parents, wisely forseeing my
future happiness in country pleasures, had early instructed me in
rural accomplishments of drinking fat ale, playing at whisk, and
smoking tobacco with my husband? or of spreading of plasters,
brewing of diet-drinks, and stilling rosemary-water, with the good
old gentlewoman my mother-in-law?
[DORIDNA: I'm sorry, madam, that it is not more in our power to
divert you; I could wish, indeed, that our entertainment were a little
less refined.   But, pray, madam, how came the poets and
philosophers, that laboured so much in hunting after pleasure, to
place it at last in a country life?]
MRS. SULLEN: [Because they wanted money, child, to find out
the pleasures of the town.] Did you ever see a poet or philosopher
worth ten thousand pounds? if you can show me such a man, I'll lay
you fifty pounds you'll find him somewhere within the weekly bills.
Not that I disapprove rural pleasures, as the poets have painted them;
in their landscape, every Phillis has her Corydon, every murmuring
stream, and every flowery mead, gives fresh alarms to love.
Besides, you'll find, that their couples were never married:—but
yonder I see my Corydon, and a sweet swain it is, Heaven knows!
Come, Dorinda, don't be angry, he's my husband, and your brother;
and, between both, is he not a sad brute?
[DORINDA: I have nothing to say to your part of him, you're the
best judge.]
MRS. SULLEN: O sister, sister! if ever you marry, beware of a
sullen, silent sot, one that's always musing, but never thinks.
There's some diversion in a talking blockhead; and since a woman

must wear chains, I would have the pleasure of hearing 'em rattle a little. Now you shall see, but take this by the way. He came home this morning at his usual hour of four, wakened me out of a sweet dream of something else, by tumbling over the tea-table, which he broke all to pieces; after his man and he had rolled about the room, like sick passengers in a storm, he comes flounce into bed, dead as a salmon into a fishmonger's basket; his feet cold as ice, his breath hot as a furnace, and his hands and his face greasy as his flannel night-cap. O matrimony! He tosses up the clothes with a barbarous swing over his shoulders, disorders the whole economy of my bed, leaves me half naked, and my whole night's comfort is the tuneable serenade of that wakeful nightingale, his nose! Oh, the pleasure of counting the melancholy clock by a snoring husband! But now, sister, you shall see how handsomely, being a well-bred man, he will beg my pardon.

MISS SARA SAMPSON
by Gotthold Ephraim Lessing
translated by Ernest Bell

A room in an inn - Sara (20's)

Sara, a young lady of pure heart, has run away with the disreputable Mellefont. Here, she tells Mellefont of a dream.

SARA: Do not accuse Heaven! It has left the imagination in our power. She is guided by our acts; and when these are in accordance with our duties and with virtue the imagination serves only to increase our peace and happiness. A single act, Mellefont, a single blessing bestowed upon us by a messenger of peace, in the name of the Eternal One, can restore my shattered imagination again. Do you still hesitate to do a few days sooner for love of me, what in any case you mean to do at some future time? Have pity on me, and consider that, although by this you may be freeing me only from torments of the imagination, yet these imagined torments are torments, and are real torments for her who feels them. Ah! could I but tell you the terrors of the last night half as vividly as I have felt them. Wearied with crying and grieving— my only occupations—I sank down on my bed with half-closed eyes. My nature wished to recover itself a moment, to collect new tears. But hardly asleep yet, I suddenly saw myself on the steepest peak of a terrible rock. You went on before, and I followed with tottering, anxious steps, strengthened now and then by a glance which you threw back upon me. Suddenly I heard behind me a gentle call, which bade me stop. It was my father's voice—I unhappy one, can I forget nothing which is his? Alas if his memory renders him equally cruel service; if he too cannot forget me!—But he has forgotten me. Comfort! cruel comfort for his Sara!—But, listen, Mellefont! In turning round to this well-known voice, my foot slipped; I reeled, and was on the point of falling down the precipice, when just in time, I felt myself held back by one who resembled myself. I was just returning her my passionate thanks, when she drew a dagger from her bosom. "I saved you," she cried, "to ruin you!" She lifted her armed hand—and—! I awoke with the blow. Awake, I still felt all the pain which a mortal stab must give, without the pleasure which it brings—the hope for the end of grief in the end of life.

MISS SARA SAMPSON
by Gotthold Ephraim Lessing
translated by Ernest Bell
A room in an inn - Marwood (30's)

Marwood is a woman who was cast aside by the rakish
Mellefont and who has attempted to take the life of Sara, his
new lover. Here she rages about her base intentions and
threatens to take her own life as well.

MARWOOD: What does the excitable girl mean? Would that she
speak the truth, and that I approached her with murderous hand! I
ought to have spared the dagger until now, fool that I was! What
delight to be able to stab a rival at one's feet in her voluntary
humiliation! What now? I am detected. Mellefont may be here this
minute. Shall I fly from him? Shall I await him? I will wait, but
not in idleness. Perhaps the cunning of my servant will detain him
long enough? I see I am feared. Why do I not follow her then?
Why do I not try the last expedient which I can use against her?
Threats are pitiable weapons; but despair despises no weapons,
however pitiable they may be. A timid girl, who flies stupid and
terror-stricken from my mere name, can easily take dreadful words
for dreadful deeds. But Mellefont! Mellefont will give her fresh
threats. He will! Perhaps he will not! Few things would have been
undertaken in this world, if men had always looked to the end. And
am I not prepared for the most fatal end? The dagger was for
others, the drug is for me! The drug for me! Long carried by me
near my heart, it here awaits its sad service; here, where in better
times I hid the written flatteries of my lovers,—poison for us equally
sure if slower. Would it were not destined to rage in my veins only!
Would that a faithless one—why do I waste my time in wishing?
Away! I must not recover my reason nor she hers. He will dare
nothing, who wishes to dare in cold blood!

SHE STOOPS TO CONQUER
by Oliver Goldsmith
18th century London - Miss Hardcastle (20's)

This young lady posed as a barmaid in order to win the man she
loved. Here, she addresses the audience on the different ages of
women.

MISS HARDCASTLE: Well, having stoop'd to conquer with
   success,
And gain'd a husband without aid from
   dress,
Still as a bar-maid, I could wish it too,
As I have conquer'd him to conquer you:
And let me say, for all your resolution,
That pretty bar-maids have done execu-
   tion.
Our life is all a play, composed to please;
"We have our exits and our entrances."
The first act shows the simple country
   maid,
Harmless and young, of everything
   afraid;
Blushes when hired, and with unmeaning
   action,
"I hopes as how to give you satisfaction."
Her second act displays a livelier scene,—
Th' unblushing bar-maid of a country
   inn,
Who whisks about the house, at market
   caters,
Talks loud, coquets the guests, and
   scolds the waiters.
Next the scene shifts to town, and there
   she soars,
The chop-house toast of ogling *connois-*

seurs;

On 'squires and cits she there displays her
arts,

And on the gridiron broils her lovers'
hearts;

And, as she smiles, her triumphs to complete,

E'en common-councilmen forget to eat.

The fourth act shows her wedded to the
'squire,

And madam now begins to hold it higher;

Pretends to taste, at operas cries *caro,*

And quits her Nancy Dawson for Che
Faro:

Doats upon dancing, and in all her pride,

Swims round the room, the Heinel of Cheapside:

Ogles and leers with artificial skill,

Till having lost in age the power to kill,

She sits all night at cards, and ogles at
spadille.

Such, through our lives, th' eventful history—

The fifth and last act still remains for
me.

The bar-maid now for your protection
prays,

Turns female barrister, and pleads for
Bayes.

THE BARBER OF SEVILLE
by Pierre Augustin Caron de Beaumarchais
translated by W.R. Taylor
The house of Bartholo, a physician, in Seville - Rosine (18-20)

Here, the innocent young Rosine entertains a lecherous count
with a song of springtime.

ROSINE: *(sings)* When hand in hand
Through Springtime's wonderland
   Come love and flowers,
Then all things new life do take,
Tender and adoring young hearts awake;
   Then speed the hours
   In green twined bowers
Where swain and shepherdess their tasks
   forsake.

Far rove the flocks
O'er hills and mossy rocks,
   The hamlet spurning.
Sweetly the cries of young lambs re-
   sound
As gaily they gambol and sprightly they
   bound.
   The blossoms are blowing,
   All things else growing
And rejoicing in sweet pleasures new
   found.

Faithful dogs keep
Watch o'er the sheep
   That nearby graze.
While Lindor passion-shaken,
His gentle charge quite forsaken,
   Of his shepherdess dreams

THE BARBER OF SEVILLE

Nor ever deems
Life possible without love's thrilling
    maze.

Far from her mother
To the green recess
    Where waits her anxious lover,
Singing and tripping goes the sweet shep-
    herdess.
By this device does love entice
    And snare the pretty rover.
    But will singing save her?

The melodious reeds
She lists and heeds;
Filled with alarms
From her budding charms
From the birds as they sweetly sing,
The poor little thing,
    The timorous maid,
As she trips along,
    Trembles afraid.

From his hidden retreat
Her advance to meet
    Lindor springs forward.
With rapture he has kissed her;
She, well content, and with armorous joy
    pent,
    In feigned anger rails,
    And loudly wails,
So that he will appease her.

Now come the sighs, the moving fears,

THE BARBER OF SEVILLE

The promises, the joyful tears,
Tender dalliance, amorous treasures,
Gentle repartee, and lover's pleasures.
    The shepherdess her anger has forgot-
    ten quite:
    In love's name all kisses are right.

If some wretched intruding swain
Awkwardly surprises their lover's re-
    treat,
With one accord the height of indifference
    they feign,
And his early departure they greet:
    Restraint can naught but heighten
    The pleasures of love we feel.

EGMONT
by Johann Wolfgang Goethe
translated by Anna Swanwick
Brussels - Clara (20's)

Clara's lover is Count Egmont, the brave leader of the rebellion against Spanish rule in the Netherlands. Clara has heard rumors of his capture and here anxiously awaits their confirmation.

CLARA: *(enters from her chamber with a lamp and a glass of water; she places the glass upon the table and steps to the window).* Brackenburg, is it you? What noise was that? No one yet? No one! I will set the lamp in the window, that he may see that I am still awake, that I still watch for him. He promised me tidings. Tidings? horrible certainty!—Egmont condemned!—What tribunal has the right to summon him?—And they dare to condemn him!—Is it the king who condemns him, or the duke? And the Regent withdraws herself! Orange hesitates, as do all his friends!—Is this the world, of whose fickleness and treachery I have heard so much, and as yet experienced nothing? Is this the world?—Who could be so base as to bear malice against one so dear? Could villainy itself be audacious enough to overwhelm with sudden destruction the object of a nation's homage? Yet so it is—it is—Oh Egmont, I held thee safe before God and man, safe as in my arms! What was I to thee? Thou hast called me thine, my whole being was devoted to thee. What am I now? In vain I stretch out my hand to the toils that environ thee. Thou helpless, and I free!—Here is the key that unlocks my chamber door. My going out and my coming in, depend upon my own caprice; yet, alas, to aid thee I am powerless!—Oh bind me that I may not go mad; hurl me into the deepest dungeon, that I may dash my head against the damp walls, groan for freedom, and dream how I would rescue him if fetters did not hold me bound. —Now I am free, and in freedom lies the anguish of impotence.— Conscious of my own existence, yet unable to stir a limb in his behalf, alas! even this insignificant portion of thy being, thy Clara, is, like thee, a captive, and separated from thee, consumes her expiring energies in the agonies of death.—I hear a stealthy step,—a cough—Brackenburg,—'tis he!—Kind, unhappy man, thy destiny remains ever the same; thy love opens to thee the door at night,—alas! to what a doleful meeting.

THE INSPECTOR GENERAL
by Nikolai Gogol
translated by Robert Saffron

A Russian village - 1830's - The Locksmith's Wife (30-50)

Believing a young bureaucrat to the inspector general, the wife of the local locksmith wastes no time in complaining to him about the corrupt mayor, who has forced her husband to join the army against her wishes.

LOCKSMITH'S WIFE: Beggin' your mercy, I want to complain against the Mayor! I hope the Lord curses him with every kind of disease he can dig up, so that crook and his children and his uncles and his aunts never have any luck in anything!

[HLESTAKOV: Really? Why?]

LOCKSMITH'S WIFE: Why, that grafter stuck my man into the army—and it ain't his turn yet! Besides, it's against the law because my man's *married!* To me!

[HLESTAKOV: But how could the Mayor do that?]

LOCKSMITH'S WIFE: [He done it anyhow, the swindler.] He just done it! I hope God blasts him good in this world *and* the next! And his aunt—if he *had* an aunt—let every kind of sickness shrivel her up! And his father—if he *had* a father and he's alive—let him rot to death, the rat! I hope he chokes forever and ever, that thief! They shoulda took the tailor's son, the drunk, but his family slipped the Mayor a big bribe. So he snatched Panteleyeva's son, but his old lady sent around three bolts of cloth to the Mayor's wife. So he picks on *me!* "What do you need a husband for?" he says. "He's no use to you." Well, I'm the one that oughta know if he's any use or not! Then he says, "Your husband is a crook. It don't matter if he ain't stole nothin' yet, he sure will someday. So what's the difference if they take him now or next year?" What am I gonna do without my dear husband? You stinkin' Mayor! I hope not one of your family wakes up tomorrow to see God's blessed light. And your mother-in-law—if you *have* a mother-in-law—

[HLESTAKOV: Now! now! That's enough! *(He dismisses her. To the other.)* Now, what do you have to complain about?]

LOCKSMITH'S WIFE: *(as she goes out)* Don't forget me, little father. And bless you.

188

MARIA MAGDALENA
by Friedrich Hebbel
translated by Carl Richard Mueller

A town of moderate size, the cabinet maker's house - Klara (20-30)

Klara reveals her love and concern for her mother as she
watches the older woman walk to church.

KLARA: *(watching her from the window)* There she goes. Three
times I dreamt I saw her lying in a coffin, and then...why must these
terrible dreams clothe themselves in our fears and frighten us so! I
must never again pay attention to dreams, never be happy because
of a good one, and so never be afraid because of the bad one that
always follows. How firm and steady she walks. I wonder who'll
be the first to meet her? I know it doesn't mean anything, but...
(startled) the grave-digger! He's climbing out of a grave that he's
just finished digging. She's bowing to him and smiling as she looks
down into that hole. And now she throws her bouquet of flowers
into it and goes into the church *(The sounds of a choral heard)*
They're singing: "Now thank we all our God." *(She folds her
hands)* God, my God, if my mother had died, I would never have
found peace again. *(She looks toward heaven)* But Thou art
merciful, Thou art compassionate! I wish that I believed like the
Catholics do, so that I could offer something to You. I would take
all the money I have and buy You a lovely golden heart and wreathe
it with roses. Our pastor says that offerings mean nothing to You
because all things are Yours already, and we ought not to want to
give You what You already possess. But everything in this house
belongs to my father, and still it makes him happy when for his
birthday I buy him a handkerchief with his own money and put it on
his plate to surprise him. Yes, and then he always honors my gift
by wearing it only on the highest holydays, at Christmas or
Pentecost. One time I saw a tiny Catholic girl carrying cherries to
the altar as an offering. It made me so happy to watch her! They
were the first cherries of the year that they'd given the child, and I
saw how much she wanted to eat them. But still she fought against

MARIA MAGDALENA

her innocent desire, and to put all end to her temptation she put down the cherries so quickly that the priest who had just raised the chalice looked at her so threateningly that he frightened the child away. And then I saw the Blessed Virgin smiling so tenderly above the altar, as if she wanted to step down out of her frame to hurry after the child and kiss her. I did it for her—Leonard's coming!

THE DEMI-MONDE
by Alexandre Dumas Fils
translated by Harold Harper
19th century Paris - Suzanne (20-30)

Here, the manipulative Suzanne chastises her ex-lover for treating her poorly.

SUZANNE: Now, let us talk seriously. By what right have you behaved this way? In what way can you reproach me? If Monsieur de Nanjac were an old friend of yours, a childhood comrade, or a brother, I might see, but you have known him scarcely a week or ten days. If you were disinterested, too, I might understand, but are you quite sure you haven't been prompted by wounded pride? I know you don't love me, but a man always rather resents being told by a woman who once loved him that she no longer does so. Simply because you happened to make love to me and because I was confiding enough to believe you, because I thought you an honorable man, because I loved you, perhaps, are you going to be an obstacle to the happiness of my whole life? Did I compromise you? ruin you? Did I even deceive you? I will admit,—I must admit, because it's true—that I am not worthy on moral grounds, of the name and position I aspire to; but is it your place—you helped make me unworthy!—to close to me the honorable path I have chosen to tread? No, my dear Olivier, it's not right; when a person has himself succumbed to certain weaknesses, he ought not to forge weapons and use them against those with whom he has sinned. A man who has been loved, no matter how little, provided the love was based neither on interest nor calculation, is under an eternal obligation to the woman, and he should remember that no matter how much he does for her, he can never hope to repay her.

THE THUNDERSTORM
by Alexander Ostrovsky
translated by Florence Whyte and George Rapall Noyes
The town of Kalinov, Russia - 19th century - Katerina (20-30)

Katerina here confides to her sister-in-law that she is unhappy
with the confinements of married life and longs for the freedom
that she enjoyed as a young girl.

KATERINA: I tell you: I wonder why people can't fly like birds.
You know, sometimes I imagine that I am a bird. When you stand
on a hill, you just long to fly. You feel that you could take a run,
raise your arms, and fly away. Do you want to try it now?

(She starts to run.)

[VARVARA: What notions you get!]

KATERINA: *(sighing)* I used to be so lively! I have shriveled up
completely in your house.

[VARVARA: Don't you think I can see that?]

KATERINA: I was so different. I just lived and didn't worry about
anything; I was like an uncaged bird. My mother was so fond of
me; she dressed me up like a doll and never made me work; I used
to do just as I pleased. Do you know how I used to live before I
was married? I'll tell you all about it. I used to get up early. In
summer I would go to the spring, and bathe; I would carry back
water and sprinkle all the flowers in the house. I had lots and lots
of flowers. Then mamma and I would go to church, and the
pilgrims too—our house used to be full of pilgrims and holy women.
When we came from church we would sit down to some work,
usually gold thread on velvet, and the pilgrims would begin to tell
about the places they had visited, what they had seen, and the lives
of saints, or they would sing songs. So the time would pass till
dinner. Then the older people would lie down to rest, and I would
walk about the garden. Then I would go to vespers, and in the
evening there would be more stories and songs. It was so nice!

[VARVARA: But it is just the same at our house.]

KATERINA: But everything here seems to be under restraint. I used to love dearly to go to church! It seemed as if I were in heaven. I could see no one, I didn't notice the time passing and I didn't hear when the service ended. It seemed all to have happened in a second. Mamma said that every one used to look at me and wonder what was happening to me. And you know, on sunny days a shining column came down from the dome and in it smoke hovered like clouds and I seemed to see angels flying and singing in the column. Or else I would get up at night—we, too, used to have lamps burning everywhere at night—and I would go into some corner and pray till morning. Or early in the morning I would go into the garden when the sun was hardly up; I would fall on my knees and pray and weep, and I would not know myself why I prayed or why I wept—and so they would find me. And what I prayed about then, and what I asked for, I cannot imagine; I didn't need anything. I had enough of everything. And such dreams as I used to have, Varenka, wonderful dreams! of golden temples, or marvelous gardens where unseen voices would sing and cypress trees wafted forth their fragrance. And the mountains and trees were not the ordinary kind, but like those that are painted on the sacred images. Or I would fly and fly away through the air. And sometimes I dream now, but rarely, and then it is not the same.

[VARVARA: Why?]

KATERINA: *(after a pause)*. I shall die soon.

THE THUNDERSTORM
by Alexander Ostrovsky
translated by Florence Whyte and George Rapall Noyes
The town of Kalinov, Russia - 19th century - Katerina (20-30)

Katerina has fallen in love with young Boris and finally escapes
the suffocating confines of her husband's house. Rejected by
all, she wanders aimlessly, tortured by the knowledge of her
betrayal.

KATERINA: No, he is not to be found anywhere! What is he
doing now, poor boy? If I could only say good-bye to him, and
then—then die. Why did I lead him into misfortune? It's no easier
for me! I ought to have perished alone! But now I have ruined
myself, ruined him: I'm dishonored, he will always be under a
cloud. Yes, I'm dishonored. He's under a cloud. *(Pause.)* Can I
remember what he used to say? How he pitied me! What words did
he say? *(She clasps her head.)* I don't remember; I've forgotten it
all. The nights, the nights are so hard! They all go to bed, and I go
too; they go to sleep and I go down to my tomb. It's so terrible in
the dark! There's a noise and they sing as if they were burying
some one, only so quietly I can hardly hear it, far, far from me.
And how glad I am to see the light! But I don't want to get up—the
same people again, the same talk, the same torture. Why do they
look at me in such a way? Why don't they put people to death now?
Why have they acted in this way? In former times, they say, they
used to put people to death. They would have taken me and thrown
me in the Volga, and I should have been glad. "If we put you to
death," they say, "then your sin will be taken from you; live on and
torture yourself with your sin." I've been tortured enough for it.
Must I be tortured much longer?...What shall I live for now! What
for? I don't need anything now; nothing is dear to me, God's world
itself is not dear to me! But death does not come. You call to it,
but it does not come. Whatever I see or hear, I have the same pain
here. *(She points to her heart.)* If I could still live with him,
perhaps I should still find a little happiness. Well, well, now it's all

THE THUNDERSTORM

the same; I've already destroyed my soul. How I long for him!
How I long for him! If I cannot see you more, then at least hear my
voice from afar. Wild winds, carry to him my sorrow and longing!
Heavens, I am weary, weary! *(She walks to the bank and cries
aloud.)* My joy, my life, my soul, I love you! Answer me!

MISS JULIE
by August Strindberg
translated by Evert Sprinchorn
The Count's manor house - 19th century Sweden - Julie (20's)

Julie has impulsively agreed to run away with Jean, a servant in
her father's employ. When Jean kills her pet canary so as not
to be burdened with its cage on their flight, Julie erupts with
long-repressed rage.

MISS JULIE: *(screaming)* Kill me too! Kill me! You can kill an
innocent creature without turning a hair—then kill me. Oh how I
hate you! I loathe you! There's blood between us. I curse the
moment I first laid eyes on you! I curse the moment I was
conceived in my mother's womb. *(She approaches the chopping
block as if drawn to it against her will)* No, I don't want to go yet.
I can't.—I have to see.—Shh! I hear a carriage coming! *(She listens
but keeps her eyes fastened on the chopping block and cleaver)* You
don't think I can stand the sight of blood, do you? You think I'm so
weak! Oh, I'd love to see your blood and your brains on that
chopping block. I'd love to see the whole of your sex swimming in
a sea of blood just like that. I think I could drink out of your skull.
I'd like to bathe my feet in your ribs! I could eat your heart roasted
whole!—You think I'm weak! You think I loved you because my
womb hungered for your seed. You think I want to carry your
brood under my heart and nourish it with my blood! Bear your child
and take your name! Come to think of it, what is your name
anyway? I've never heard your last name. You probably don't even
have one. I'd be Mrs. Doorkeeper or Madame Floorsweeper. You
dog with my name on your collar—you lackey with my initials on
your buttons! Do you think I'm going to share you with my cook
and fight over you with my maid?! Ohhh!—You think I'm a coward
who's going to run away. No, I'm going to stay. Come hell or
high water, I don't care! My father will come home—find his
bureau broken into—his money gone. Then he rings—on that bell—
two rings for the valet. And then he sends for the sheriff—and I tell

196

him everything. Everything! Oh it'll be wonderful to have it all over...if only it will be over....He'll have a stroke and die. Then there'll be an end to all of us. There'll be peace...and quiet...forever....His coat of arms will be broken on the coffin; the Count's line dies out. But the valet's line will continue in an orphanage, win triumphs in the gutter and end in jail!

LADY WINDERMERE'S FAN
by Oscar Wilde
Late 19th century London - Lady Windermere (20-30)

When she discovers her husband's infidelity, Lady Windermere decides to run away with the notorious Lord Darlington. Here, she anxiously awaits his arrival.

LADY WINDERMERE: *(standing by the fireplace).* Why doesn't he come? This waiting is horrible. He should be here. Why is he not here, to wake by passionate words some fire within me? I am cold—cold as a loveless thing. Arthur must have read my letter by this time. If he cared for me, he would have come after me, would have taken me back by force. But he doesn't care. He's entrammeled by this woman—fascinated by her—dominated by her. If a woman wants to hold a man, she has merely to appeal to what is worst in him. We make gods of men, and they leave us. Others make brutes of them and they fawn and are faithful. How hideous life is!...Oh! it was mad of me to come here, horribly mad. And yet which is the worst, I wonder, to be at the mercy of a man who loves one, or the wife of a man who in one's own house dishonours one? What woman knows? What woman in the whole world? But will he love me always, this man to whom I am giving my life? What do I bring him? Lips that have lost the note of joy, eyes that are blighted by tears, chill hands and icy heart. I bring him nothing. I must go back—no; I can't go back, my letter has put me in their power—Arthur would not take me back! That fatal letter! No! Lord Darlington leaves England to-morrow. I will go with him—I have no choice. *(Sits down for a few moments. Then starts up and puts on her cloak.)* No, no! I will go back, let Arthur do with me what he pleases. I can't wait here. It has been madness my coming. I must go at once. As for Lord Darlington—Oh, here he is! What shall I do? What can I say to him? Will he let me go away at all? I have heard that men are brutal, horrible...Oh! *(Hides her face in her hands.)*

SALOMÉ
by Oscar Wilde
The court of Herod - Salomé (15-20)

The fickle nature of youth is well-illustrated in Salomé's immature seduction of John the Baptist.

SALOMÉ: Jokanaan!

[JOKANAAN: Who speaketh?]

SALOMÉ: I am amorous of thy body, Jokanaan! Thy body is white like the lilies of a field that the mower hath never mowed. Thy body is white like the snows that lie on the mountains of Judæa, and come down into the valleys. The roses in the garden of the Queen of Arabia are not so white as thy body. Neither the roses of the garden of the Queen of Arabia, the garden of spices of the Queen of Arabia, nor the feet of the dawn when they light on the leaves, nor the breast of the moon when she lies on the breast of the sea.... There is nothing in the world so white as thy body. Suffer me to touch thy body.

[JOKANAAN: Back! daughter of Babylon! By woman came evil into the world. Speak not to me. I will not listen to thee. I listen but to the voice of the Lord God.]

SALOMÉ: Thy body is hideous. It is like the body of a leper. It is like a plastered wall where vipers have crawled; like a plastered wall where the scorpions have made their nest. It is like a whitened sepulchre full of loathsome things. It is horrible, thy body is horrible. It is thy hair that I am enamoured of, Jokanaan. Thy hair is like clusters of grapes, like the clusters of black grapes that hang from the vine-trees of Edom in the land of the Edomites. Thy hair is like the cedars of Lebanon, like the great cedars of Lebanon that give their shade to the lions and to the robbers who would hide them by day. The long black nights, when the moon hides her face, when the stars are afraid, are not so black as thy hair. The silence that dwells in the forest is not so black. There is nothing in the world that is so black as thy hair....Suffer me to touch thy hair.

[JOKANAAN: Back, daughter of Sodom! Touch me not. Profane

not the temple of the Lord God.]

SALOMÉ: Thy hair is horrible. It is covered with mire and dust. It is like a knot of serpents coiled round thy neck. I love not thy hair…. It is thy mouth that I desire, Jokanaan. Thy mouth is like a band of scarlet on a tower of ivory. It is like a pomegranate cut in twain with a knife of ivory. The pomegranate-flowers that blossom in the gardens of Tyre, and are redder than roses, are not so red. The red blasts of trumpets that herald the approach of kings, and make afraid the enemy, are not so red. Thy mouth is redder than the feet of the doves who inhabit the temples and are fed by the priest. It is redder than the feet of him who cometh from a forest where he hath slain a lion, and seen gilded tigers. Thy mouth is like a branch of coral that fishers have found in the twilight of the sea, the coral that they keep for the kings!…It is like the vermilion that the Moabites find in the mines of Moab, the vermilion that the kings take from them. It is like the bow of the King of the Persians, that is painted with vermilion, and is tipped with coral. There is nothing in the world so red as thy mouth…. Suffer me to kiss thy mouth.

[JOKANAN: Never! daughter of Babylon! Daughter of Sodom! Never.]

SALOMÉ: I will kiss thy mouth, Jokanaan. I will kiss thy mouth.

SALOMÉ
by Oscar Wilde
The court of Herod - Salomé (15-20)

When Herod reluctantly grants her demand for the head of John
the Baptist, Salomé grieves for the loss of his life.

SALOMÉ: *(she leans over the cistern and listens).* There is no
sound. I hear nothing. Why does he not cry out, this man? Ah! if
any man sought to kill me, I would cry out, I would struggle, I
would not suffer...Strike, strike, Naaman, strike, I tell you.... No,
I hear nothing. There is a silence, a terrible silence. Ah! something
has fallen upon the ground. I heard something fall. He is afraid,
this slave. He is a coward, this slave! Let soldiers be sent. *(She
sees the PAGE OF HERODIAS and addresses him.)* Come hither,
thou wert the friend of him who is dead, wert thou not? Well, I tell
thee, there are not dead men enough. Go to the soldiers and bid
them go down and bring me the thing I ask, the thing the Tetrarch
has promised me, the thing that is mine. *(The PAGE recoils. She
turns to the SOLDIERS.)* Hither, ye soldiers. Get ye down into this
cistern and bring me the head of this man. Tetrarch, Tetrarch,
command your soldiers that they bring me the head of Jokanaan. *(A
huge black arm, the arm of the Executioner, comes forth from the
cistern, bearing on a silver shield the head of JOKANAAN.
SALOMÉ seizes it. HEROD hides his face with his cloak.
HERODIAS smiles and fans herself. The NAZARENES fall on their
knees and begin to pray.)* Ah! thou wouldst not suffer me to kiss thy
mouth, Jokanaan. Well, I will kiss it now. I will bite it with my
teeth as one bites a ripe fruit. Yes, I will kiss thy mouth, Jokanaan.
I said it; did I not say it? I said it. Ah! I will kiss it now...But,
wherefore dost thou not look at me, Jokanaan? Thine eyes that were
so terrible, so full of rage and scorn, are shut now. Wherefore are
they shut? Open thine eyes! Lift up thine eyelids, Jokanaan!
Wherefore dost thou not look at me? Art thou afraid of me,
Jokanaan, that thou wilt not look at me?...And thy tongue, that was
like a red snake darting poison, it moves no more, it speaks no

words, Jokanaan, that scarlet viper that spat its venom upon me. It is strange, is it not? How is it that the red viper stirs no longer? ...Thou wouldst have none of me, Jokanaan. Thou rejectedst me. Thou didst speak evil words against me. Thou didst bear thyself toward me as to a harlot, as to a woman that is a wanton, to me, Salomé, daughter of Herodias, Princess of Judæa! Well, I still live, but thou art dead, and thy head belongs to me. I can do with it what I will. That which the dogs leave, the birds of the air shall devour ...Ah, Jokanaan, thou wert the man that I loved alone among men. All other men were hateful to me. But thou wert beautiful! Thy body was a column of ivory set upon feet of silver. It was a garden full of doves and lilies of silver. It was a tower of silver decked with shields of ivory. There was nothing in the world so white as thy body. There was nothing in the world so black as thy hair. In the whole world there was nothing so red as thy mouth. Thy voice was a censer that scattered strange perfumes, and when I looked on thee I heard a strange music. Ah! wherefore didst thou not look at me, Jokanaan? With the cloak of thine hands and with the cloak of thy blasphemies thou didst hide thy face. Thou didst put upon thine eyes the covering of him who would see his God. Well, thou has seen thy God, Jokanaan, but me, me, thou didst never see. If thou hadst seen me thou hadst loved me. I saw thee, and I loved thee. Oh, how I loved thee! I love thee yet, Jokanaan, I love only thee... I am athirst for thy beauty; I am hungry for thy body; and neither wine nor apples can appease my desire. What shall I do now, Jokanaan? Neither the floods nor the great waters can quench my passion. I was a princess, and thou didst scorn me. I was chaste, and thou didst fill my veins with fire...Ah! ah! wherefore didst thou not look at me? If thou hadst looked at me thou hadst loved me. Well I know that thou wouldst have loved me, and the mystery of love is greater than the mystery of death.

MAGDA
by Herman Sudermann
translated by Charles Edward Amory Winslow
A provincial 19th cenutry European town - Magda (30-40)

When her performance in a concert brings her back to her childhood home, Magda finds that reconciliation with her family is impossible. When her father threatens to kill her unless she marries the man who fathered her child, she explodes with years of stored anger.

MAGDA: *(After a short silence.)* My poor, dear papa! Why do you torture yourself so? And do you think that I will let myself be contrained by locked doors? You cannot believe it.

[SCHWARTZE: You will see.]

MAGDA: *In growing excitement.)* And what do you really want of me? Why do you trouble yourself about me? I had almost said, what have you all to do with me?

[SCHWARTZE: That you will see.]

MAGDA: You blame me for living out my life without asking you and the whole family for permission. And why should I not? Was I not without family? Did you not send me out into the world to earn my bread, and then disown me because the way in which I earned it was not to your taste? Whom did I harm? Against whom did I sin? Oh, if I had remained the daughter of the house, like Marie, who is nothing and does nothing without the sheltering roof of the home, who passes straight from the arms of her father into the arms of her husband; who receives from the family life, thought, character, everything—yes, then you would have been right. In such a one the slightest error would have ruined everything—conscience, honor, self-respect. But I? Look at me. I was alone. I was as shelterless as a man knocked about in the world, dependent on the work of my own hands. If you give us the right to hunger—and I have hungered—why do you deny us the right to love, as we can find it, and to happiness, as we can understand it?

[SCHWARTZE: You think, my child, because you are free and a

great artist, that you can set at naught—]

MAGDA: Leave art out of the question. Consider me nothing more than the seamstress, the servant-maid who seeks, among strangers, the little food and the little love she needs. See how much the family with its morality demands from us! It throws us on our own resources, it gives us neither shelter nor happiness, and yet, in our loneliness, we must live according to the laws which it has planned for itself alone. We must still crouch in the corner, and there wait patiently until a respectful wooer happens to come. Yes, wait. And meanwhile the war for existence of body and soul is consuming us. Ahead we see nothing but sorrow and despair, and yet shall we not once dare to give what we have of youth and strength to the man for whom our whole being cries? Gag us, stupefy us, shut us up in harems or in cloisters—and that perhaps would be best. But if you give us our freedom, do not wonder if we take advantage of it.

UNCLE VANYA
Scenes from Country Life
by Anton P. Chekhov
translated by Marian Fell
A country estate - 19th century Russia - Helena (20's)

Here, Helena takes a moment to muse over the unrequited love of her friend, Sonia, as well as her own forbidden feelings for the fiery Dr. Astroff.

HELENA: *(Alone.)* There is no greater sorrow than to know another's secret when you cannot help them. *(In deep thought.)* He is obviously not in love with her but why shouldn't he marry her? She is not pretty, but she is so clever and pure and good she would make a splendid wife for a country doctor of his years. *(A pause.)* I can understand how the poor child feels. She lives here in this desperate loneliness with no one around her except these colorless shadows that go mooning about talking nonsense and knowing nothing except that they eat, drink and sleep. Among them appears from time to time this Dr. Astroff, so different, so handsome, so interesting, so charming. It is like seeing the moon rise on a dark night. Oh, to surrender oneself to his embrace! To lose oneself in his arms! I am a little in love with him myself! Yes, I am lonely without him, and when I think of him I smile. That Uncle Vanya says I have the blood of a nixie in my veins: "Give rein to your nature for once in your life!" Perhaps it is right that I should. Oh, to be free as a bird, to fly away from all your sleepy faces and your talk and forget that you have existed at all! But I am a coward, I am afraid; my conscience torments me. He comes here every day now. I can guess why, and feel guilty already; I should like to fall on my knees at Sonia's feet and beg her forgiveness, and weep.

THE DREAM PLAY
by August Strindberg
translated by Edwin Björkman
The legendary Fingal's Cave - The daughter of Indra (20's)

The daughter of the mighty god is approached by an earthly poet, who asks that she read a grievance in the form of a prayer to her father. Here, she reads it aloud.

THE DAUGHTER: *(Receives the roll, but reads without looking at it.)* Well, by me it shall be spoken then:

"Why must you be born in anguish?
Why O man-child, must you always
Wring your mother's heart with torture
When you bring her joy maternal,
Highest happiness yet known?
Why to life must you awaken,
Why to light give natal greeting,
With a cry of anger and of pain?
Why not meet it smiling, man-child,
When the gift of life is counted
In itself a boon unmatched?
Why like beasts should we be coming,
We of race divine and human?
Better garment craves the spirit,
Than one made of filth and blood!
Need a god his teeth be changing—"

—Silence rash one! Is it seemly
For the work to blame its maker?
No one yet has solved life's riddle.

"Thus begins the human journey
O'er a road of thorns and thistles;
If a beaten path be offered

THE DREAM PLAY

It is named at once forbidden;
If a flower you covet, straightway
You are told it is another's;
If a field should bar your progress,
And you dare to break across it,
You destroy your neighbor's harvest;
Others then your own will trample,
That the measure may be evened!
Every moment of enjoyment
Brings to some one else a sorrow,
But your sorrow gladdens no one,
For from sorrow naught but sorrow springs.

"Thus you journey till you die
And your death brings others' bread."

—Is it thus that you approach,
Son of Dust, the One Most High?

[THE POET: Could the son of dust discover
Words so pure and bright and simple
That to heaven they might ascend—?

Child of gods, wilt thou interpret
Mankind's grievance in some language
That immortals understand?]

IN THE SHADOW OF THE GLEN
by John M. Synge
A cottage, County Wicklow, Ireland - 1900's - Nora (40's)

Believing her husband to be dead, Nora tells a young admierer
of the reasons she chose to marry and her fears for the future.

NORA: What way would I live and I an old woman if I didn't
marry a man with a bit of a farm, and cows on it, and sheep on the
back hills?

[MICHEAL: *(considering),* That's true, Nora, and maybe it's no
fool you were, for there's good grazing on it, if it is a lonesome
place, and I'm thinking it's a good sum he's left behind.]

NORA: *(taking the stocking with money from her pocket, and
putting it on the table).* I do be thinking in the long nights it was a
big fool I was that time, Micheal Dara, for what good is a bit of a
farm with cows on it, and sheep on the back hills, when you do be
sitting looking out from a door the like of that door, and seeing
nothing but the mists rolling down the bog, and the mists again, and
they rolling up the bog, and hearing nothing but the wind crying out
in the bits of broken trees were left from the great storm, and the
streams roaring with the rain.

[MICHEAL: *(looking at her uneasily).* What is it ails you, this
night, Nora Burke? I've heard tell it's the like of that talk you do
hear from men, and they after being a great while on the back hills.]

NORA: *(putting out the money on the table).* It's a bad night, and
a wild night, Micheal Dara, and isn't it a great while I am at the foot
of the back hills, sitting up here boiling food for himself, and food
for the brood sow, and baking a cake when the night falls? *(She
puts up the money, listlessly, in little piles on the table).* Isn't it a
long while I am sitting here in the winter and the summer, and the
fine spring, with the young growing behind me and the old passing,
saying to myself one time, to look on Mary Brien who wasn't that
height *(holding out her hand),* and I a fine girl growing up, and
there she is now with two children, and another coming on her in
three months or four. *(She pauses.)*

IN THE SHADOW OF THE GLEN

[MICHEAL: *(moving over three of the piles).* That's three pounds we have now, Nora Burke.]

NORA: *(continuing in the same voice).* And saying to myself another time, to look on Peggy Cavanagh, who had the lightest hand at milking a cow that wouldn't be easy, or turning a cake, and there she is now walking round on the roads, or sitting in a dirty old house, with no teeth in her mouth, and no sense and no more hair than you'd see on a bit of a hill and they after burning the furze from it.

THE PASSION FLOWER
by Jacinto Benavente
translated by John Garrett Underhill
A farmhouse in Castille - 1920's - Raimunda (40-50)

When she discovers that her husband is in love with her
daughter, and has murdered the young woman's fiance,
Raimunda confronts him with his crimes.

RAIMUNDA: Yes, give yourself up! Bring shame and ruin on this
house, drag my daughter's honor in the dust and mire of the village!
I should have been the law to you; you ought to have thought of me.
Do you suppose that I believe in these tears because this is the first
time I ever saw you cry? Better you had cried your eyes out the day
that wicked thought first entered your mind rather than have turned
them where you had no right. Now you cry—but what am I to do?
Look at me. Nobody knows what I have been through. It could not
be worse. I want to forget but I must think—think how I can hide
the shame which has fallen on this house, keep it out of men's sight,
prevent a man from being dragged from this house to prison—a man
I brought into it to be a father to my child! This was my father's
house; here my brothers lived with the fear of God in their hearts
and from it they went to serve their King or to marry or to till other
fields by their labor. When they re-entered these doors it was with
the same honor with which they went forth. Don't cry; don't hang
your head. Hold it high, as I do. In a few minutes the officers will
be here to trap us all. Though the house burn, and they are in it,
they shall not smell the smoke. Dry your eyes; you have wept
blood. Take a sip of water—I wish it was poison. Don't drink so
fast; you are overheated. The thorns have torn your skin. You
deserved knives. Let me wash you off; it makes my blood creep to
look at you.

210

THE ADDING MACHINE
by Elmer Rice
An unspecified city in the 1920's - Mrs. Zero (45)

Mrs. Zero reveals her shallow and mean nature in the following verbal assault on her resting husband.

MRS. ZERO: *(As she takes down her hair)* I'm gettin' sick o' them Westerns. All them cowboys ridin' around an' foolin' with them ropes. I don't care nothin' about that. I'm sick of 'em. I don't see why they don't have more of them stories like "For Love's Sweet Sake." I like them sweet little love stories. They're nice an' wholesome. Mrs. Twelve was sayin' to me only yesterday, "Mrs. Zero," says she, "what I like is one of them wholesome stories, with just a sweet, simple little love story." "You're right, Mrs. Twelve," I says. "That's what I like, too." They're showin' too many Westerns at the Rosebud. I'm gettin' sick of them. I think we'll start goin' to the Peter Stuyvesant. They got a good bill there Wednesday night. There's a Chubby Delano comedy called "Sea-Sick." Mrs. Twelve was tellin' me about it. She says it's a scream. [They're havin' a picnic in the country and they sit Chubby next to an old maid with a great big mouth. So he gets sore an' when she ain't lookin' he goes and catches a frog and drops it in her clam chowder. An' when she goes to eat the chowder the frog jumps out of it an' right into her mouth. Talk about laugh! Mrs. Twelve was tellin' me she laughed so she nearly passed out. He sure can pull some funny ones. An' they got that big Grace Darling feature, "A Mother's Tears." She's sweet. But I don't like her clothes. There's no style to them. Mrs. Nine was tellin' me she read in *Pictureland* that she ain't livin' with her husband. He's her second, too. I don't know whether they're divorced or just separated. You wouldn't think it to see her on the screen. She looks so sweet and innocent. Maybe it ain't true. You can't believe all you read. They say some Pittsburgh millionaire is crazy about her and that's why she ain't livin' with her husband. Mrs. Seven was tellin' me her brother-in-law has a friend that used to go to school with Grace]

THE ADDING MACHINE

Darling. He says her name ain't Grace Darling at all. Her right name is Elizabeth Dugan, he says, an' all them stories about her gettin' five thousand a week is the bunk, he says. She's sweet though. Mrs. Eight was tellin' me that "A Mother's Tears" is the best picture she ever made. "Don't miss it, Mrs. Zero," she says. "It's sweet," she says. "Just sweet and wholesome. Cry!" she says, "I nearly cried my eyes out." There's one part in it where this big bum of an Englishman—he's a married man, too—an' she's this little simple country girl. An' she nearly falls for him, too. But she's sittin' out in the garden, one day, and she looks up and there's her mother lookin' at her, right out of the clouds. So that night she locks the door of her room. An' sure enough, when everybody's in bed, along comes this big bum of an Englishman an' when she won't let him in what does he do but go an' kick open the door. "Don't miss it, Mrs. Zero," Mrs. Eight was tellin' me. It's at the Peter Stuyvesant Wednesday night, so don't be tellin' me you want to go to the Rosebud. The Eights seen it downtown at the Strand. They go downtown all the time. Just like us—nit! I guess by the time it gets to the Peter Stuyvesant all that part about kickin' in the door will be cut out. Just like they cut out that big cabaret scene in "The Price of Virtue." They sure are pullin' some rough stuff in the pictures nowadays. "It's no place for a young girl," I was tellin' Mrs. Eleven, only the other day. An' by the time they get uptown half of it is cut out. But you wouldn't go downtown—not if wild horses was to drag you. You can wait till they come uptown! Well, I don't want to wait, see? I want to see 'em when everybody else is seein' them an' not a month later. Now don't go tellin' me you ain't got the price. You could dig up the price all right, all right, if you wanted to. I notice you always got the price to go to the ball game. But when it comes to me havin' a good time then it's always: "I ain't got the price, I gotta start savin'." A fat lot you'll ever save! I got all I can do now makin' both ends meet an' you talkin' about savin'. *(She seats herself on a chair and begins removing her shoes and stockings.)* An' don't go pullin' that stuff about bein'

THE ADDING MACHINE

tired. "I been workin' hard all day. Twice a day in the subway's enough for me." Tired! Where do you get that tired stuff, anyhow? What about me? Where do I come in? Scrubbin' floors an' cookin' your meals an' washin' your dirty clothes. An' you sittin' on a chair all day, just addin' figgers an' waitin' for five-thirty. There's no five-thirty for me. I don't wait for no whistle. I don't get no vacations neither. And what's more I don't get no pay envelope every Saturday night neither. I'd like to know where you'd be without me. An' what have I got to show for it?—slavin' my life away to give you a home. What's in it for me, I'd like to know? But it's my own fault, I guess. I was a fool for marryin' you. If I'd 'a' had any sense, I'd 'a' known what you were from the start. I wish I had it to do over again, I hope to tell you. You was goin' to do wonders, you was! You wasn't goin' to be a bookkeeper long— oh, no, not you. Wait till you got started—you was goin' to show 'em. There wasn't no job in the store that was too big for you. Well, I've been waitin'—waitin' for you to get started—see? It's been a good long wait, too. Twenty-five years! An' I ain't seen nothin' happen. Twenty-five years in the same job. Twenty-five years tomorrow! You're proud of it, ain't you? Twenty-five years in the same job an' never missed a day! That's somethin' to be proud of, ain't it? Sittin' for twenty-five years on the same chair, addin' up figures. What about bein' store-manager? I guess you forgot about that, didn't you? An' me at home here lookin' at the same four walls an' workin' my fingers to the bone to make both ends meet. Seven years since you got a raise! An' if you don't get one tomorrow, I'll bet a nickel you won't have the guts to go an' ask for one. I didn't pick much when I picked you, I'll tell the world. You ain't much to be proud of. *(She rises, goes to the window, and raises the shade. A few lighted windows are visible on the other side of the closed court. Looking out for a moment.)* She ain't walkin' around tonight, you can bet your sweet life on that. An' she won't be walkin' around any more nights, neither. Not in this house, anyhow. *(She turns away from the window.)* The dirty bum! The

213

idea of her comin' to live in a house with respectable people. They should 'a' gave her six years, not six months. If I was the judge I'd of gave her life. A bum like that. *(She approaches the bed and stands there a moment.)* I guess you're sorry she's gone. I guess you'd like to sit home every night an' watch her goin's-on. You're somethin' to be proud of, you are! *(She stands on the bed and turns out the light...A thin stream of moonlight filters in from the court. The two figures are dimly visible. MRS. ZERO gets into bed.)* You'd better not start nothin' with women, if you know what's good for you. I've put up with a lot, but I won't put up with that. I've been slavin' away for twenty-five years, makin' a home for you an' nothin' to show for it. If you was any kind of a man you'd have a decent job by now an' I'd be gettin' some comfort out of life— instead of bein' just a slave, washin' pots an' standin' over the hot stove. I've stood it for twenty-five years an' I guess I'll have to stand it twenty-five more. But don't you go startin' nothin' with women— *(She goes on talking as the curtain falls.)*

SAINT JOAN
by G.B. Shaw
The chamber of the accessors - 1431 - Joan (20)

Here, the maid of Orleans tells her captors that it is they who
are ruled by the devil and not she.

JOAN: Yes: they told me you were fools *(the word gives great
offence)*, and that I was not to listen to your fine words nor trust to
your charity. You promised me my life; but you lied *(indignant
exclamations)*. You think that life is nothing but not being stone
dead. It is not the bread and water I fear: I can live on bread: when
have I asked for more? It is no hardship to drink water if the water
be clean. Bread has no sorrow for me, and water no affliction. But
to shut me from the light of the sky and the sight of the fields and
flowers; to chain my feet so that I can never again ride with the
soldiers nor climb the hills; to make me breathe foul damp darkness,
and keep from me everything that brings me back to the love of God
when your wickedness and foolishness tempt me to hate Him: all this
is worse than the furnace in the Bible that was heated seven times.
I could do without my warhorse; I could drag about in a skirt; I
could let the banners and the trumpets and the knights and soldiers
pass me and leave me behind as they leave the other women, if only
I could still hear the wind in the trees, the larks in the sunshine, the
young lambs crying through the healthy frost, and the blessed
blessed church bells that send my angel voices floating to me on the
wind. But without these things I cannot live; and by your wanting
to take them away from me, or from any human creature, I know
that your counsel is of the devil, and that mine is of God.

JUNO AND THE PAYCOCK
by Sean O'Casey
A tenement house, Dublin - 1922 - Mrs. Tancred (50-70)

When her son is killed by soldiers, Mrs. Tancred shares her grief with her friends.

MRS. TANCRED: An' I'll go on livin' like a pauper. Ah, what's the pains I suffered bringin' him into the world to carry him to his cradle, to the pains I'm sufferin' now, carryin' him out o' the world to bring him to his grave!

[MARY: It would be better for you not to go at all, Mrs. Tancred, but to stay at home beside the fire with some o' the neighbors.]

MRS. TANCRED: I seen the first of him, an' I'll see the last of him.

[MRS. BOYLE: You'd want a shawl, Mrs. Tancred, it's a cowld night, an' the win's blowin' sharp.]

[MRS. MADIGAN: *(Rushing out.)* I've a shawl above.]

MRS. TANCRED: Me home is gone, now; he was me only child an' to think that he was lyin' for a whole night stretched out on the side of a lonely counthry lane, with his head, his darlin' head, that I ofen kissed an' fondled, half hidden in the wather of a runnin' brook. An' I'm told he was the leadher of the ambush where me nex' door neighbor, Mrs. Mannin', lost her Free State soldier son. An' now here's the two of us oul' women, standin' one on each side of a scales o' sorra, balanced be the bodies of our two dead darlin' sons. *(MRS. MADIGAN returns, and wraps a shawl around her.)* God bless you, Mrs. Madigan... *(She moves slowly toward the door.)* Mother o' God, Mother o' God, have pity on the pair of us!...O Blessed Virgin, where were you when me darlin' son was riddled with bullets, when me darlin' son was riddled with bullets! ...Sacred Heart of the Crucified Jesus, take away our hearts o' stone ...an' give us hearts o' flesh!...Take away this murdherin' hate...an' give us Thine own eternal love!

When her son brings home his new wife, Mrs. Phelps pleads
with her new daughter-in-law to leave her some place in David's
heart.

MRS. PHELPS: Very well, I shall try, my dear. Now you must
listen to me and try to understand me....Look at me. What do you
see? Simply—David's mother. I can't say of you that you're simply
David's wife, because, clearly, you're many things beside that. But
I am simply his mother....I think, as I talk to you, that I belong to
a dead age. I wonder if you think that? In my day, we considered
a girl immensely courageous and independent who taught school or
gave music lessons. Nowadays, girls sell real estate and become
scientists and think nothing of it. Give us our due, Christina. We
weren't entirely bustles and smelling salts, we girls who did not go
into the world. We made a great profession which I fear may be in
some danger of vanishing from the face of the earth. We made a
profession of motherhood. That may sound old-fashioned to you.
Believe me, it had its value. I was trained to be a wife that I might
become a mother. *(CHRISTINA is about to protest. MRS. PHELPS
stops her.)* Your father died of his investigations of a dangerous
disease. You called that splendid of him, didn't you? Would you
say less of us who gave our lives to being mothers? Mothers of
sons, particularly. Listen to me, Christina. David was five, Rob
only a little baby, when my husband died. I'd been married six
years, not so very happily. I was pretty, as a girl, too. Very pretty.
(This thought holds her for a second.) For twenty-four years, since
my husband died, I've given all my life, all my strength to Dave and
Rob. They've been my life and my job. They've taken the place of
husband and friends both, for me. Where do I stand, now? Rob is
marrying. David is married already. This is the end of my life and
my job...Oh, I'm not asking for credit or praise. I'm asking for
something more substantial. I'm asking you, my dear, dear

Christina, not to take all my boy's heart. Leave me, I beg you, a little, little part of it. I've earned that much. I'm not sure I couldn't say that you owe me that much—as David's mother. I believe I've deserved it. Don't you think I have?

THE SILVER CORD
by Sidney Howard
Suburban America - 1920's - Christina (20-30)

Christina fears that David's mother is ruining their marriage and tells him so.

CHRISTINA: *(Gravely, but with steadily increasing fervor.)* Have you ever thought what it would be like to be trapped in a submarine in an accident? I've learned tonight what that kind of panic would be like. I'm in that kind of panic now this minute. I've been through the most awful experience of my life tonight. And I've been through it alone. I'm still going through it alone. It's pretty awful to have to face such things alone.... No, don't interrupt me. I've got to get this off my chest. Ever since we've been married I've been coming across queer rifts in your feeling for me, like arid places in your heart. Such vast ones, too! I mean, you'll be my perfect lover one day, and the next I'll find myself floundering in sand, and alone, and you nowhere to be seen. We've never been really married, Dave. Only now and then, for a little while at a time, between your retirements into your arid places.... I used to wonder what you did there. At first, I thought you did your work there. But you don't. Your work's in my part of your heart, what there is of my part. Then I decided the other was just No-Man's Land. And I thought: little by little, I'll encroach upon it and pour my love upon it, like water on the western desert, and make it flower here and bear fruit there. I thought: then he'll be all alive, all free and all himself; not partly dead and tired and blind; not partly someone else—or nothing. You see, our marriage and your architecture were suffering from the same thing. They only worked a little of the time. I meant them both to work all the time. I meant you to work all the time and to win your way, *all* your way, Dave, to complete manhood. And that's a good deal farther than you've got so far.... Then we came here and this happened with Hester and your brother and you just stepped aside and did nothing about it! You went to bed. You did worse than that. You retired into your private wastes and sat tight

219

THE SILVER CORD

....I've shown you what you should do and you won't see it. I've called to you to come out to me, and you won't come. So now I've discovered what keeps you. Your mother keeps you. It isn't No-Man's Land at all. It's your mother's land. Arid, sterile, and your mother's! You won't let me get in there. Worse than that, you won't let life get in there! Or she won't!...That's what I'm afraid of, Dave—your mother's hold on you. And that's what's kept me from getting anywhere with you, all these months. I've seen what she can do with Robert. And what she's done to Hester. I can't help wondering what she may not do with you and to me and to the baby. That's why I'm asking you to take a stand on this business of Hester's, Dave. You'll never find the right any clearer than it is here. It's a kind of test case for me. Don't you see? What you decide about this is what you may, eventually, be expected to decide about...about our marriage.

THE SKIN OF OUR TEETH
by Thornton Wilder
A commuter's home in New Jersey - 1940's - Sabrina (30's)

Here, the family maid awaits the return of the master of the
house while treating the audience to an entertaining introduction
to his family.

SABRINA: Oh, oh, oh! Six o'clock and the master not home yet.
Pray God nothing serious has happened to him crossing the
Hudson River. If anything happened to him, we would certainly be
inconsolable and have to move into a less desirable residence district.

The fact is I don't know what'll become of us. Here it is the
middle of August and the coldest day of the year. It's simply
freezing; the dogs are sticking to the sidewalks; can anybody explain
that? No.

But I'm not surprised. The whole world's at sixes and sevens,
and why the house hasn't fallen down about our ears long ago is a
miracle to me. *(A fragment of the right wall leans precariously over
the stage. SABRINA looks at it nervously and it slowly rights itself)*
Every night this same anxiety as to whether the master will get home
safely: whether he'll bring home anything to eat. In the midst of life
we are in the midst of death, a truer word was never said. *(The
fragment of scenery flies up into the lofts. SABRINA is struck dumb
with surprise, shrugs her shoulders and starts dusting MR.
ANTROBUS' chair, including the under side)* Of course Mr.
Antrobus is a very fine man, an excellent husband and father, a
pillar of the church and has all the best interests of the community
at heart. Of course every muscle goes tight every time he passes a
policeman; but what I think is that there are certain charges that
ought not to be made and I think I may add, ought not to be allowed
to be made; we're all human; who isn't? *(She dusts MRS.
ANTROBUS' rocking chair)* Mrs. Antrobus is as fine a woman as
you could hope to see. She lives only for her children; and if it
would be any benefit to her children she'd see the rest of us

stretched out dead at her feet without turning a hair,—that's the truth. If you want to know anything more about Mrs. Antrobus just go and look at a tigress and look hard.

As to the children—

Well, Henry Antrobus is a real clean-cut American boy. He'll graduate from High School one of these days if they make the alphabet any easier.—Henry, when he has a stone in his hand has a perfect aim; he can hit anything from a bird to an older brother—Oh! I didn't mean to say that!—but it certainly was an unfortunate accident and it was very hard getting the police out of the house.

Mr. and Mrs. Antrobus' daughter is named Gladys. She'll make some good man a good wife some day if he'll just come down off the movie screen and ask her.

So here we are!

We've managed to survive for some time now, catch as catch can, the fat and the lean, and if the dinosaurs don't trample us to death, and if the grasshoppers don't eat up our garden, we'll all live to see better days, knock on wood.

Each new child that's born to the Antrobuses seems to them to be sufficient reason for the whole universe's being set in motion; and each new child that dies seems to them to have been spared a whole world of sorrow, and what the end of it will be is still very much an open question.

We've rattled along, hot and cold, for some time now— *(A portion of the wall above the door, right, flies up into the air and disappears)* —and my advice to you is not to inquire into why or whither, but just enjoy your ice cream while it's on your plate, that's my philosophy.

Don't forget that a few years ago we came through the depression by the skin of our teeth! One more tight squeeze like that and where will we be? *(This is a cue line. SABRINA looks angrily at the kitchen door and repeats)*...we came through the depression by the skin of our teeth, one more tight squeeze like that and where will we be? *(Flustered, she looks through the opening in the right wall; then goes to the window and reopens the Act)* Oh, oh, oh! Six o'clock and the master not home yet! Pray God nothing has happened to him crossing the Hudson. Here it is the middle of August and the coldest day of the year. It's simply freezing; the dogs are sticking. One more tight squeeze like that and where will we be?

THE SKIN OF OUR TEETH
by Thornton Wilder
A commuter's home in New Jersey - 1940's - Fortune Teller (30-60)

Here, an earthy Fortune Teller observes that it's much easier to
tell a person's future than their past.

FORTUNE TELLER: I tell the future. Keck. Nothing easier.
Everybody's future is in their face. Nothing easier.

But who can tell your past—eh? Nobody!

Your youth,—where did it go? It slipped away while you
weren't looking. While you were asleep. While you were drunk.
Puh! You're like our friends, Mr. and Mrs. Antrobus; you lie
awake nights trying to know your past. What did it mean? What
was it trying to say to you?

Think! Think! Split your heads. I can't tell the past and neither
can you. If anybody tries to tell you the past, take my word for it,
they're charlatans! Charlatans! But I can tell the future. *(She
suddenly barks at a passing chair-pusher)* Apoplexy! *(She returns
to the audience)* Nobody listens.—Keck! I see a face among you
now—I won't embarrass him by pointing him out, but, listen, it may
be you: Next year the watchsprings inside you will crumple up.
Death by regret,—Type Y. It's in the corners of your mouth.
You'll decide that you should have lived for pleasure, but that you
missed it. Death by regret,—Type Y.... Avoid mirrors. You'll try
to be angry,—but no!—no anger. *(far forward, confidentially)* And
now what's the immediate future of our friends the Antrobuses? Oh,
you've seen it as well as I have, keck,—that dizziness of the head;
that Great Man dizziness? The inventor of beer and gunpowder?
The sudden fits of temper and then the long stretches of inertia?
"I'm a sultan; let my slave-girls fan me?"

You know as well as I what's coming. Rain. Rain. Rain in
floods. The deluge. But first you'll see shameful things—shameful
things. Some of you will be saying: "Let him drown. He's not
worth saving. Give the whole thing up." I can see it in your faces.
But you're wrong. Keep your doubts and despairs to yourselves.

SKIN OF OUR TEETH

Again there'll be the narrow escape. The survival of a handful. From destruction,—total destruction. *(She points sweeping with her hand to the stage)* Even of the animals, a few will be saved: two of a kind, male and female, two of a kind.

CAMINO REAL
by Tennessee Williams
A fantasy limbo called "Camino Real" - Marguerite (indefinite age)

A woman trapped in limbo cautions her male companion not to fall in love with her.

MARGUERITE: Oh, Jacques, we're used to each other, we're a pair of captive hawks caught in the same cage, and so we've grown used to each other. That's what passes for love at this dim, shadowy end of the Camino Real... What are we sure of? Not even of our existence, dear comforting friend! And whom can we ask the questions that torment us? "What is this place?" "Where are we?"—a fat old man who gives sly hints that only bewilder us more, a fake of a Gypsy squinting at cards and tea-leaves. What else are we offered? The never-broken procession of little events that assure us that we and strangers about us are still going on! Where? Why? and the perch that we hold is unstable! We're threatened with eviction, for this is a port of entry and departure, there are no permanent guests! And where else have we to go when we leave here? Bide-a-While? "Ritz Men Only"? Or under that ominous arch into Terra Incognita? We're lonely. We're frightened. We hear the Streetcleaners' piping not far away. So now and then, although we've wounded each other time and again— we stretch out hands to each other in the dark that we can't escape from—we huddle together for some dim-communal comfort—and that's what passes for love on this terminal stretch of the road that used to be royal. What is it, this feeling between us? When you feel my exhausted weight against your shoulder—when I clasp your anxious old hawk's head to my breast, what is it we feel in whatever is left of our hearts? Something, yes, something—delicate, unreal, bloodless! The sort of violets that could grow on the moon, or in the crevices of those far away mountains, fertilized by the droppings of carrion birds. Those birds are familiar to us. Their shadows inhabit the plaza. I've heard them flapping their wings like old charwomen beating worn-out carpets with gray brooms... But tenderness, the violets in the mountains—can't break the rocks!
226

CAT ON A HOT TIN ROOF
by Tennessee Williams
"Big Daddy" Pollitt's home, Mississippi - 1950's - Margaret (30's)

Maggie's husband, an alcoholic ex-football star, has lost interest in her sexually. Here, she tries to rekindle their relationship by making him jealous.

MARGARET: You know, our sex life didn't just peter out in the usual way, it was cut off short, long before the natural time for it to, and it's going to revive again, just as sudden as that. I'm confident of it. That's what I'm keeping myself attractive for. For the time when you'll see me again like other men see me. Yes, like other men see me. They still see me, Brick, and they like what they see. Uh-huh. Some of them would give their—Look, Brick!
(She stands before the long oval mirror, touches her breast and then her hips with her two hands.)
    How high my body stays on me!—No'hing has fallen on me—not a fraction...
(Her voice is soft and trembling: a pleading child's. At this moment as he turns to glance at her—a look which is like a player passing a ball to another player, third down and goal to go—she has to capture the audience in a grip so tight that she can hold it till the first intermission without any lapse of attention.)
Other men still want me. My face looks strained, sometimes, but I've kept my figure as well as you've kept yours, and men admire it. I still turn heads on the street. Why, last week in Memphis everywhere that I went men's eyes burned holes in my clothes, at the country club and in restaurants and department stores, there wasn't a man I met or walked by that didn't just eat me up with his eyes and turn around when I passed him and look back at me. Why, at Alice's party for her New York cousins, the best lookin' man in the crowd—followed me upstairs and tried to force his way in the powder room with me, followed me to the door and tried to force his way in!

CAT ON A HOT TIN ROOF
by Tennessee Williams
"Big Daddy" Pollitt's house, Mississippi - 1950's - Margaret (30's)

Brick holds Maggie responsible for the death of his best friend.
Here, she passionately confronts his accusations.

MARGARET: Brick, don't brain me yet, let me finish!—I know, believe me I know, that it was only Skipper that harbored even any *unconscious* desire for anything not perfectly pure between you two!—Now let me skip a little. You married me early that summer we graduated out of Ole Miss, and we were happy, weren't we, we were blissful, yes, hit heaven together ev'ry time that we loved! But that fall you an' Skipper turned down wonderful offers of jobs in order to keep on bein' football heroes—pro-football heroes. You organized the Dixie Stars that fall, so you could keep on bein' team-mates forever! But somethin' was not right with it!—*Me included!*—between you. Skipper began hittin' the bottle...you got a spinal injury—couldn't play the Thanksgivin' game in Chicago, watched it on TV from a traction bed in Toledo. I joined Skipper. The Dixie Stars lost because poor Skipper was drunk. We drank together that night all night in the bar of the Blackstone and when cold day was comin' up over the Lake an' we were comin' out drunk to take a dizzy look at it, I said, "SKIPPER! STOP LOVIN' MY HUSBAND OR TELL HIM HE'S GOT TO LET YOU ADMIT IT TO HIM!"—one way or another!

HE SLAPPED ME HARD ON THE MOUTH!—then turned and ran without stopping once, I am sure, all the way back into his room at the Blackstone...

—When I came to his room that night, with a little scratch like a shy little mouse at his door, he made that pitiful, ineffectual little attempt to prove that what I had said wasn't true...
(Brick strikes at her with crutch, a blow that shatters the gemlike lamp on the table.)
—In this way, I destroyed him, by telling him truth that he and his world which he was born and raised in, yours and his world, had

told him could not be told?

—From then on Skipper was nothing at all but a receptacle for liquor and drugs...

—*Who shot cock-robin? I with my—*

(She throws back her head with tight shut eyes.)

—*merciful arrow!*

(Brick strikes at her; misses.)

Missed me!—Sorry,—I'm not tryin' to whitewash my behavior, Christ, no! Brick, I'm not good. I don't know why people have to pretend to be good, nobody's good. The rich or the well-to-do can afford to respect moral patterns, conventional moral patterns, but I could never afford to, yeah, but—I'm honest! Give me credit for just that, will you *please?*—Born poor, raised poor, expect to die poor unless I manage to get us something out of what Big Daddy leaves when he dies of cancer! But Brick?!—*Skipper is dead! I'm alive!* Maggie the cat is—

(Brick hops awkwardly forward and strikes at her again with his crutch.)

—alive! I am alive, alive! I am...

THE APOLLO OF BELLAC
from the French of Jean Giraudoux
adapted by Maurice Valency
International Bureau of Investigations, Paris - 1950's - Agnes (20-30)

When a timid woman is visited by the god of beauty, she speaks
to him of her less-than-beautiful life.

AGNES: You dazzle my eyes.

[MAN: But your heart sees me.]

AGNES: I'm not so sure. Do not count on me too much, God of
Beauty. My life is small. My days are long, and when I come back
to my room each evening, there are five flights to climb in the
greasy twilight amid smells of cooking. These five flights mark the
beginning and the end of every event of my life, and oh, if you
knew, Apollo, how lonely I am! Sometimes I find a cat waiting in
a doorway. I kneel and stroke it for a moment, we purr together
and it fills the rest of my day with joy. Sometimes I see a milk
bottle that has fallen on its side. I set it right and the gesture
comforts me. If I smell gas in the hallway I run and speak to the
janitor. It is so good to speak to someone about something.
Between the second story and the third, the steps sag. At this
turning one abandons hope. At this turning one loses one's balance,
and catches at the bannister, gasping with the anguish of those more
fortunate ones who clutch at the rail on the heaving deck of a ship.
That is my life, Apollo, a thing of shadows and tortured flesh. That
is my conscience, Apollo, a staircase full of stale odors. If I hesitate
to see you as you are, O beautiful god, it is because I need so much
and I have so little and I must defend myself.

[MAN: But I have rescued you, Agnes. You possess the secret.]

AGNES: I know. From now on, my staircase will be new and full
of light, the treads carpeted in velvet and adorned with initials. But
to climb it with you would be unthinkable. Go away, God of
Beauty. Leave me for always.

[MAN: You wish that?]

AGNES: If you were merely a handsome man, Apollo, thick and

human in your flesh, with what joy I would take you in my arms! How I would love you! But you are too brilliant and too great for my staircase. I would do better to look at my diamond. Go, Apollo. Go away. Before I open my eyes, I implore you, vanish.

GLORY IN THE FLOWER
by William Inge
The Paradise roadhouse - 1950's - Jackie (30-40)

When Bus returns to the small midwestern town of his
childhood, he is confronted by Jackie, the woman he left behind.

JACKIE: *(now it is her turn to feel embarrassed).* No. I never got
married, Bus.

[BUS: *(his face now turns serious. Something has been recalled).*
Oh...]

JACKIE: *(quick to reassure him).* Oh, but I *could* have, Bus.
Lotsa times. I dated Bunny Byram after you left...

[BUS: Old Bunny?]

JACKIE: He wanted to marry me, but he drank so much.

[BUS: Yah. You stayed outa trouble there.]

JACKIE: And I went with Dick Parsons a while, but I never really
cared for him...much. And I got a boy friend now. Yes. His name
is Gerald Baker. He sells dental supplies. I met him once in Dr.
Millard's office, and he called me for a date that night. He's an
awful nice fellow and a peck of fun. He wants to marry me...and
I've been thinking it over. He...he's...well, he's nothing like you,
Bus. But I seem to like him *more* every time we go out together.
He...he seems to...to really like me. *(She gives a little laugh of
embarrassment.)*

[BUS: *(feeling a little morose).* Well...I used to wonder about you
at times...*you* know.]

JACKIE: People really were very nice about it, Bus. After a while.
At first they weren't. I mean...when I first came back to town, lotsa
people wouldn't speak to me, and I didn't go to church or anything
because I knew how all the women would look at me, but I got busy
right away. I teach piano lessons. That was the only thing I knew
how to do very well, was play the piano, and I had to earn a living.
I didn't have many pupils at first, but people soon forgot and now
I got all the pupils I can take care of, and no one ever tries to

remind me...

[BUS: *(this is very hard for him to ask)*.   What...what ever happened to...]

JACKIE: It was a little girl, Bus. I never saw her. I figured the best thing I could do for her was to give her to that place in Chicago. They see that the babies are adopted by nice families and ...Well, they took her from me the very first thing. The nurse said it would be easier that way, if I never saw her. So I never did.

PERMISSIONS ACKNOWLEDGMENTS

234

236